You Got Me!—Florida

Rob Lloyd

Illustrations by Tim Lloyd

Pineapple Press, Inc.

Sarasota, Florida

For Beverly and Gabriella

Inquiries should be addressed to:
Pineapple Press, Inc.
P.O. Box 3899
Sarasota, FL 34230

www.pineapplepress.com

Source photographs courtesy of the Florida State Archives
Airplane *Impervo* used with permission of Gus Miller

Library of Congress Cataloging-in-Publication Data

Lloyd, Rob.
        You got me!—Florida / Rob Lloyd. — 1st ed.
    p. cm.
    Includes bibliographical references and index.
    ISBN 1-56164-183-9 (alk. paper)
    1. Florida Miscellanea. 2. Questions and answers. I. Title.
    F311.6.L58   1999
    975.9—dc21   99-20444
                                    CIP

First Edition
10 9 8 7 6 5 4 3 2 1

Illustrations by Tim Lloyd
Cover design by Carol Tornatore
Interior design by Steve Duckett
Composition by Sandra Wright's Designs
Printed by Edwards Brothers, Lillington, North Carolina

Acknowledgments

The author wishes to thank *Flamingo Fortune* producers Gary Dawson, Leslie Wilson, and Andy Felsher. Thanks to Catharine Hohmeister and the reference department of the State Library of Florida, as well as the staff of the Tampa-Hillsborough County Public Library, Joe Stines, Director. Source photographs courtesy of the Florida State Archives, with grateful acknowledgment to Joan Morris and the staff. Airplane *Impervo* used with the kind permission of sculptor Gus Miller. Special thanks to Justine Rathbun and Charlotte Sheedy.

About the Author

Rob Lloyd is the writer behind TV game show classics such as *Family Feud* with Richard Dawson, *To Tell The Truth,* Burt Reynolds's *Win, Lose or Draw,* and many others. Rob Lloyd divides his time between Los Angeles and Tampa, where he lives with his wife and daughter.

Table of Contents

Introduction

In 1514 when the first tour group took a wrong turn on the way to Bimini and bumped into a flowery place they called Florida, little did they know that this dead-level limestone plateau that hangs oddly off North America would one day be the top tourist stop in the world and one of the fastest growing states in the country.

Today, Florida hosts as many as 47 million visitors a year from around the nation and around the world. In addition, newcomers arrive in Florida at a brisk clip; over a million and a half of today's Floridians (11%) are new to the state since 1990 (me among them). Early in the 21st century, Florida is projected to overtake New York as the third most populous state in the U.S.

It is for visitors and recent arrivals alike that *You Got Me!—Florida* has been created. Not a tourist guide, but a reference book unlike others you may be used to. Sure, the index is full of many of the same subjects found in other books of Florida trivia, but this book differs from other reference books in at least one important way: *You Got Me!— Florida* is a reference that's meant to be fun.

The material in this book represents the work of many writers, and any credit for a fascinating nugget should be given to the source listed. I have included only material I think is true and comes from reliable sources, but for any inadvertent errors I put the blame on myself, if only for carrying bad information. I offer my apology and will make corrections in future editions. A lot of material has been processed to put this book together. I extend my sincere appreciation to those hundreds of authors and journalists whose work I pored through and hope that I have not done them any disservice.

I would like to hear from you what you like or don't like about this book. You can e-mail me at yougotmefl@aol.com or drop me a line at P.O. Box 13844, Tampa, FL, 33681-0844. My ultimate wish is for you to have fun with this information, so please enjoy.

Rob Lloyd

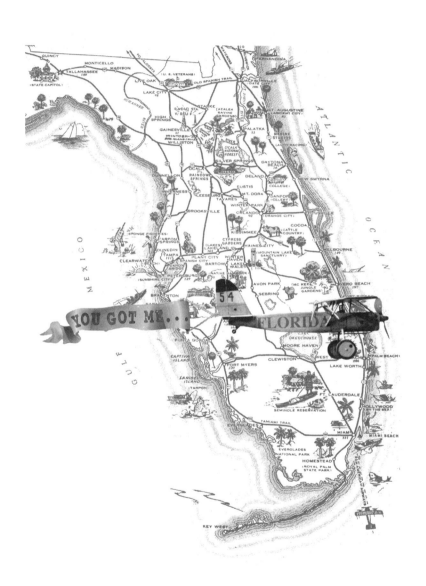

Chapter 1

Changes in Latitude—
Florida Geography

Due south

Longitudinaliy speaking, Jacksonville is more or less a straight shot
south of the city of—you got me! Is it. . . ?

1. **Portsmouth, NH**
2. **New York City**
3. **Cleveland, OH**

Cleveland. And Pensacola falls in line under Chicago. *Florida
Handbook 1997–1998*

From sea to shining sea

You got me how far is the farthest point you can get from salt water
and still be in Florida! Is it. . . ?

1. **30 miles**
2. **70 miles**
3. **110 miles**

70 miles. *Florida Handbook 1997–1998*

As old as the hills

About 180 million to 250 million years ago, the mega-landmass called
Pangaea began to break up and make room for the Atlantic. But you
got me what continent drifted away and left behind Florida! Was it. . . ?

1. **Europe**
2. **South America**
3. **Africa**

The Floridan Plateau was part of what is today Africa. Paleozoic
stones in Florida are spitting images of sandstones in the
Mauritanide Mountains in Africa. *Some Kind of Paradise by Mark
Derr and Florida Ramble by Alex Shoumatoff*

Ain't no mountain high enough

Alaska boasts the *highest* high peak in the 50 states: Mount McKinley, at 20,320 feet. Florida, on the other hand, has the lowest high peak in the nation: Britton Hill. But you got me how high that is! Is it. . . ?

    1. **345 feet**
    2   3,450 feet
    3. 13,450 feet

At 345 feet, Britton Hill is little more than a beauty mark in the Panhandle. *St. Petersburg Times 9-19-82*

Ain't no river wide enough

An often repeated factoid is that only 2 rivers in the world flow north: the Nile and one Florida river—but you got me which one! Is it. . . ?

    1. **The Suwannee**
    2. **The St. Johns**
    3. **The Withlacoochee**

The St. Johns River, so they say; but there are more than 2. The Cuyahoga and the Tennessee flow north, not to mention a bunch of rivers that flow into the Arctic Ocean (e.g., the Pechora, Kolyma, Yama, Lena, Dvina, and so on). *Florida Times-Union and Jacksonville Journal 6-19-77*

BONUS St. Johns question

Over the course of the St. Johns River's run from the Brevard County swamps to the Atlantic, the river has an average fall of—you got me! Is it. . . ?

    1. **Less than an inch per mile**
    2. **About a foot every mile**
    3. **About 16 inches every mile**

Less than an inch per mile: a slope so slight that it drains behind the Atlantic Coastal Ridge and hence flows north. The St. Johns is the longest Florida river at between 273 and 318 miles, depending on where you put the headwaters (a matter of some dispute). *Florida Times-Union and Jacksonville Journal 6-19-77, Encyclopedia Britannica, Florida Handbook 1997–1998*

You got me which is the greatest number! Is it. . . ?

    1. **The stars in the Milky Way**

2. The gallons of water the present Florida population will consume in a lifetime
3. The gallons of water in the Florida aquifer

The aquifer is estimated to hold 1 quadrillion gallons of water; there are in the neighborhood of 1 billion stars in the galaxy. The average person consumes in the neighborhood of 16,000 gallons of water in a lifetime. Multiply that by the Florida population of 14.4 million and you get 180.4 billion gallons. *[tampatrib.com]*, *Encyclopedia Britannica, and Trivial Conquest*

Far out
You got me which is farthest from the state capital, Tallahassee! Is it. . . ?
1. Georgia
2. New Orleans
3. Miami

Miami is about 500 miles south; New Orleans is about 400 miles west; Georgia is only about 20 miles from Tallahassee. *Tallahassee Democrat 12-17-67*

Trickle-down effect
A waterfall—a rare Florida sight—can be seen at Falling Waters State Park, south of Chipley, which is also the site of the first attempt to find something in Florida—but you got me what! Was it. . . ?
1. Oil
2. The "Ma" Barker Gang
3. The rare Florida panther

Oil. Within the park area was the 1st (unproductive) search for oil under Florida. Oil was discovered in Florida near Sunniland, in Collier County. *Know Florida (State of Florida) and The Florida Park Board 8-11-67*

DeFuniak Springs in Walton County has a spring that is a perfect mile in circumference. It is also 1 of only 2 towns in the nation that is named after someone who was—you got me! Is it. . . ?
1. A civil engineer
2. A psychic
3. A known felon

Frederick de Funiak was a civil engineer with the L&N Railroad and won the honor of having the town named for him in a coin toss (or a throw of the dice). The other town is Port Jervis, NY, named for John Bloomfield Jervis, chief engineer on the Erie Canal project. *Tampa Times 6-24-73*

The harder they fall
Although results are inconclusive, experts in 1982 noted that 95% to 98% of sinkholes open up during—you got me! Is it. . . ?
1. Underground nuclear testing
2. Sunspot activity
3. A new or full moon

The moon either in its full or new phase. *Tampa Times 7-27-82*

If a tree fell in the woods
In March 1937 Oliver Chalifoux of the National Park Service came upon a fallen tree in the woods north of Marianna. He checked around the base and got a 1st look at—you got me! Was it. . . ?
1. A "Bigfoot"-type creature called the Bardin Booger
2. Underground caverns
3. The burial chamber of Ponce de León

The Florida Caverns. Over 1,000 years ago Native Americans used the deeper recesses of the caves for shelter during severe weather. During the Civil War Battle of Marianna, women and children took refuge there. *Tampa Tribune 9-30-62 and 6-11-78*

Go jump in a whatever
Around 1870, Lake Worth stopped being a lake—but you got me what it is now! Is it. . . ?
1. A bay
2. A lagoon
3. A river

Around 1870 some of the early settlers cut an inlet from the north end of freshwater Lake Worth to the ocean and the seawater flowed in, turning the lake into an 18-mile-long lagoon. *Did You Know by Wilma Spencer (Library of Congress, 1964) and WPA Guide to Florida*

You'd have to go to a point approximately 12 miles north-northwest of Brooksville, in Hernando County, if you wanted to stand on—you got me! Is it. . . ?

1. The highest point in the state
2. The farthest inland point in the state
3. The geographic center of the state

It's the approximate geographic center of Florida. *U.S. Department of the Interior Geological Survey*

Pardon our dust
The ground under the Tampa Bay area is clay and dirt for about 100 feet. But you got me what's under that! Is it. . . ?
1. Molten metallic iron
2. Limestone
3. Magma

There's about 3,000 feet of limestone saturated with water: the aquifer. *[tampatrib.com]*

A chip off the old block
About 30 or 40 million years ago, the Florida peninsula was an island—but you got me the name given to the seaway that separated it from the North American mainland! Was it. . . ?
1. The Gulf of Florida
2. The Suwannee Straits
3. The Mississippi Seaway

Suwannee Straits. *USF Magazine 9-83*

Lake Alachua, near Gainesville, and Paynes Prairie, near Gainesville, have something in common—but you got me what! Is it. . . ?
1. They're the last habitats of the elusive Florida mink
2. They're ghost towns
3. They're the same place

It's "Lake Alachua" when it fills with water (a lake large enough to support steamer traffic) and "Paynes Prairie" (as it is today) when the water suddenly vanishes underground, which it did in 1823, 1870, and 1892. *Florida's Natural Wonders 1926 and WPA Guide to Florida*

Worlds apart
The farthest distance between 2 points in all the United States is the 5,852 miles between Log Point, Elliot Key, Florida, and—you got me! Is it. . . ?

1. Kure Island, Hawaii
2. Cape Wrangell, Alaska
3. West Quoddy Head, Maine

Kure Island, Hawaii. Cape Wrangell is a little closer at 5,495 miles away. West Quoddy Head isn't even in the running. *U.S. Department of the Interior Geological Survey*

A hot tip

You got me what state in the continental U.S. is closest to the equator! Is it. . . ?
1. Arizona
2. Texas
3. Florida

The equator is 1,700 miles away, but it's Florida all right. *Florida Handbook 1997–1998*

Last and Least

Rudy Slough is the shortest one of these in Florida—but you got me what! Is it a. . . ?
1. River
2. Native resident
3. Railroad

 Rudy Slough is a river four-tenths of a mile long. *Florida Handbook 1997–1998*

Chapter 2

First Things First— Florida Firsts

Bring the house down

What are believed to be the 1st prefab houses in America were built in Fairfield, Maine, and shipped aboard 4 schooners to Fort Myers in 1885. But you got me whom they were built for! Was it. . . ?
1. Henry Flagler
2. Thomas Edison
3. Chief Osceola

Edison. *Thomas A. Edison Winter Home & Museum brochure*

On November 22, 1901, at the Fairgrounds on North Main Street in Jacksonville, an important 1st was seen in Florida—but you got me what! Was it the 1st. . . ?
1. Grapefruit
2. College football game
3. Flamingo

Florida Agricultural College of Lake City (later UF at Gainesville) played Stetson in the state's 1st intercollegiate football game. *Go Gators! The Official History of University of Florida Football 1889–1967*

In Manatee County, a pioneer woman named Mrs. Julia Atzeroth, best known as "Madame Joe," was the woman behind the 1st one of these in America—but you got me what! Was it. . . ?
1. The 1st house of ill repute
2. The 1st tourist trap
3. The 1st pound of homegrown coffee

In 1880 Madam Joe sent the 1st pound of U.S.-grown coffee to the Commissioner of Agriculture; she got $10 for it. *Tampa Tribune 8-15-54*

Boy and girl, circa 1950

On the air
The 1st airplane flight from the U.S. to a foreign country left Key West on May 17, 1913—but you got me what country it flew to! Was it. . . ?
1. Cuba
2. Mexico
3. Jamaica

Havana, Cuba. *Tampa Morning Tribune 12-14-52*

Start spreading the news
According to a Miami newspaper, in May 1887 Miami had no saloons, but the only one of these systems south of St. Augustine—you got me what! Was it. . . ?
1. A mass transit system
2. A sewer system
3. A judicial system

Sewer system. *Miami 1909 by Thelma Peters*

Keel moose and squirrel
Florida was the 1st state to enact a law limiting the number hunters could take. But you got me what creature the nation's 1st bag limit was put on! Was it. . . ?
1. Ducks
2. Wild turkeys
3. Pelicans

Turkeys. *Cycle of a Century in Game Legislation in Florida*

Power to the people
The 1st electric lights in Florida are believed to be those in Jacksonville in 1883—but you got me what got lit up! Was it a. . . ?
1. Railroad station
2. Hotel
3. University

The St. James Hotel. *Florida Handbook 1997–1998*

In 1970 the largest nongovernmental construction project in America was—you got me! Was it. . . ?

1. The space shuttle vehicle assembly building
2. Disney World
3. The Cross-Florida barge canal

Disney World. *Florida's Disney World: Promises and Problems by Leonard E. Zehnder*

Dancing in the street

In 1988 a Guinness world record was set when 119,000 (est.) dancers lined up at a Miami Sound Machine concert, at Miami's annual Calle Ocho Festival—but you got me what dance they did! Was it. . . ?
1. Mambo
2. Samba
3. Conga

Gloria Estefan and the Miami Sound Machine's "Conga" was the 1st hit to appear at the same time on Billboard's pop, black, Latin, and dance charts. *Current Biography Yearbook 1995*

You don't know what I got

You got me what Britisher H. Segrave did in Daytona on March 29, 1927! Was it. . . ?
1. Created Gerber Baby Food
2. Set the world's 1st land-speed record in excess of 200 mph
3. Became the 1st screen Tarzan

He drove 203.793 mph, the land-speed record sanctioned by the Fédération Internationale de l'Automobile. The next 7 records were also set at Daytona (up to 276.710 mph in 1935) before the whole show moved to the Bonneville Salt Flats, Utah. *Encyclopedia Britannica*

What's the frequency, Kenneth?

Florida's 1st TV station was WTVJ; it began broadcasting from Miami in—you got me when! Was it. . . ?
1. 1946
2. 1949
3. 1953

1949. *Miami in Our Own Words by Nancy Acrum and Rich Bard, Eds.*

The white zone is for loading, unloading, and getting loaded only

Located in the center of the main terminal at Orlando International, passengers can look through 6-foot windows and see the 1st of these located in an airport—but you got me what! Is it a. . . ?

1. Taxidermist
2. Microbrewery
3. Penguin exhibit

The Shipyard Brewing Company operates the 1st microbrewery located in an airport. *Greater Orlando Aviation Authority press release*

Let's make a deal

In 1956 Alcoa chairman Arthur Vining Davis made the costliest single land transaction to date in Florida history when he laid out $22.5 million for—you got me! Was it a. . . ?

1. Hotel
2. Stadium
3. Cruise-ship terminal

Davis picked up the Boca Raton Hotel and Club. *Who Was Who in Florida by Henry S. Marks*

Aren't you kind of glad they did?

Taylor County can boast the 1st organized effort to do away with something in 1919—but you got me what! Was it. . . ?

1. Illiteracy
2. Mosquitoes
3. Segregation

Taylor County initiated the 1st mosquito control effort in 1919. The 1st mosquito control district was established in 1925 in Indian River County. *Florida Health Notes July 1970*

Thank you for holding

The 1st one in Jacksonville (and probably in Florida) went from the corner of Pine and Bay Streets to the foot of Laura Street in 1878—but you got me what! Was it. . . ?

1. The 1st cable car
2. The 1st sewer pipe
3. The 1st telephone

The 1st phone went from the office of A. M. Beck to the Inland Navigation Co. (Useless phone trivia: In 1880 Jax had 34 phones and 2 boy operators; the 1st female operator, Grace McDaniels, came on in 1884.) *Dinner program honoring Pioneer Telephone Subscribers of Jacksonville, FL 1880 on 12-21-26*

🎣 BONUS phone question

Florida's 1st telephone exchange started in 1880, with men serving as operators until 1884, when women took over. But you got me what those 1st female phone operators were called! Were they. . . ?
1. Hello Girls
2. Stewardesses
3. Wire Ladies

Hello Girls. *Florida Handbook 1997–1998*

Extra, extra, read all about it

You got me what the state's 1st daily newspaper was! Was it. . . ?
1. The *Miami Gazette*
2. The *St. Augustine Gazette*
3. The *Apalachicola Gazette*

The *Apalachicola Gazette* appeared April 29, 1839. *Tampa Tribune 4-8-56*

On Friday, June 15, 1900, the 1st of these contraptions arrived in Tampa by express and was assembled at a plumbing shop. But you got me what it was! Was it. . . ?
1. A flush toilet
2. An air conditioner
3. A car

A car: The steam-powered Locomobile was owned by cigar manufacturer Eduardo Manrara (Vincente Martinez Ybor's partner). *Tampa Tribune 8-18-84 and Who Was Who in Florida by Henry S. Marks*

🎣 BONUS first car question

In August 1998 a South Korean car manufacturer opened its 1st U.S. outlet in St. Petersburg. But you got me what automaker that was! Was it. . . ?

1. Daewoo
2. Amazake
3. Daikon

Kathy Williams of St. Petersburg bought the 1st Daewoo sold in the country. (Amazake is a rice drink; Daikon is a radish). *St. Petersburg Times 8-29-98*

Little boxes made of ticky tacky

Thirty miles south of Naples, by the side of U.S. 41, the "world's smallest Post Office" (7'3" X 8'4") has served the town of Ochopee since 1934. But you got me what the building was before it was a P.O.! Was it. . . ?

1. A rabbit house
2. A horse coffin
3. A tool shed

Tool shed. Ochopee is also the supposed haunt of a swamp-dwelling Bigfoot known as the skunk ape. *Tampa Tribune 7-11-71 and St. Petersburg Times 9-18-98*

Although only the second Florida governor to die in office (1874, pneumonia), Ossian Bingley Hart lays claim to an important first, being the first governor who was—you got me! Was Hart. . . ?

1. The first born in Florida
2. The first foreign-born governor
3. The first woman governor

Hart was the first native Floridian governor. *St. Petersburg Times 12-13-98*

The chicken or the egg

You got me which one of these came 1st! Was it. . . ?

1. Florida's 1st newspaper
2. The Battle of Waterloo
3. Pop-up toasters

The *East Florida Gazette* was printed in St. Augustine in 1783; Napoleon got his in 1815; and toasters didn't pop until 1919. *Tampa Tribune 1-19-50 and People's Chronology*

On June 8, 1888, the 1st train of the Orange Belt Railway pulled into what would become St. Petersburg, Florida. The one and only passenger on the train was—you got me! Was he. . . ?

1. A retiree from New York
2. A shoe salesman from Savannah
3. A con man named Prof. Harold Hill

A shoe salesman representing a Savannah shoe company. *St. Petersburg Times 4-9-79 and 6-5-83*

Oldies but goodies

St. Augustine has long enjoyed its reputation as America's oldest continuously settled city (Pensacola was settled before St. Augustine, then abandoned), but if you include all the United States Outlying Territories, the oldest settled city is—you got me! Is it. . . ?
1. San Juan, Puerto Rico
2. Agana, Guam
3. St. Thomas, Virgin Islands

San Juan was settled 56 years before St. Augustine. *Tampa Tribune 12-15-57*

At the end of toney Key Biscayne can be found the oldest standing structure in Dade County—but you got me what it is! Is it. . . ?
1. A fort
2. A mission
3. A lighthouse

It's the Cape Florida lighthouse. *Historical Traveler's Guide to Florida by Eliot Kleinberg*

Ya ba da ba doo time
The oldest known remains of an animal killed by a human were found in the Aucilla River near Tallahassee—but you got me what kind of animal! Was it. . . ?
1. The piglike Dinohyus hollandi
2. A mastodon
3. A sabre-toothed tiger

 In 1994 a UF paleontologist discovered the tusk of a mastodon killed by humans. *Facts on File 12-22-94*

Chapter 3

Don't Get Around Much—Florida Transportation

Please return your tray tables to their full upright and locked positions: Florida flight

When you hear the whistle blowing eight to the bar
In 1914 the world's 1st scheduled commercial airline flight took off from St. Petersburg and landed in Tampa 23 minutes later. But you got me how long the train took between those cities in those days? Was it. . . ?
1. 90 minutes
2. 2½ hours
3. 9 hours

9 hours. *Tampa Tribune 11-1-96*

According to the *New York Times,* January 2, 1914, former St. Petersburg mayor A. C. Phiel was the 1st (and only) passenger aboard the world's 1st scheduled commercial airline flight—but you got me how he got the honor! Was he. . . ?
1. The next-door neighbor of pilot Tony Jannus
2. Owner of the Benoist flying boat biplane
3. Highest bidder at auction for the privilege

He paid $400 at auction for the privilege. *New York Times 1-2-14*

Pilots trained at Eglin Air Force Base for a dicey bombing mission commanded by Gen. Jimmy Doolittle. But you got me what they bombed! Was it. . . ?
1. Tokyo and other Japanese cities
2. Berlin and other German cities
3. Pearl Harbor

"REPORTS OF TRAFFIC DELAYS

NORTH AND SOUTHBOUND"

Collision of steam locomotives near Sanford, circa 1890s

16 B-25 bombers raided Japan just 4 months after the attack on Pearl Harbor. *St. Petersburg Times 8-17-81 and Encyclopedia Britannica*

Hello, I must be going
During 1 week in August 1980, a record was set when 6 planes were hijacked to Cuba (3 in one day). The planes belonged to Eastern, Republic, and Delta and were flying either to or from—you got me! Was it. . . ?
1. Miami
2. Orlando
3. Tampa

Miami. *Tampa Tribune 8-18-80*

Film at eleven
The town of Kissimmee was the 1st in the nation to pass a law regulating aircraft flying overhead. The ordinance was put into effect as a result of something that the very 1st flying machine did on its very 1st takeoff–but you got me what! Did it. . . ?
1. **Kill a cow**
2. **Clip the mayor's chimney**
3. **Fly down the main street at 10 feet off the ground**

The airplane killed a cow. *Tampa Tribune 4-6-58*

BONUS Kissimmee question
According to the town of Kissimmee's 1st-in-the-nation ordinance regulating aircraft, the speed limit for any plane flying within 50 feet over a city street was—you got me! Was it. . . ?
1. **15 mph**
2. **25 mph**
3. **35 mph**

Within 20 feet, 8 mph; within 50 feet, 15 mph; within 100 feet, 25 mph. *Tampa Tribune 4-6-53*

Liked by Ike
Jackie Cochran, a native of Muscogee, near Pensacola, was honored by President Eisenhower for being the 1st woman to fly—you got me! Was it. . . ?
1. **Through the sound barrier**
2. **In subspace**
3. **Around the world**

She broke the sound barrier in 1953 in an F-86 Sabre jet. An orphan never schooled and put to work in a Columbus, Georgia, cotton mill before age 9, Cochran wrote about it in her autobiography *The Stars At Noon. Tampa Tribune 11-22-54 and St. Petersburg Times 8-10-80*

When it absolutely, positively has to be there overnight
The world's 1st scheduled air cargo flight was on January 12, 1914, when Tony Jannus (who had piloted the 1st scheduled passenger flight only 11 days prior) flew a shipment from Tampa to St. Petersburg—but you got me what was shipped! Was it. . . ?
  1. **Prize-winning fighting cocks**
  2. **Pork**
  3. **A wedding dress**

Smoked ham and bacon shipped to St. Petersburg grocer L. C. Heffner. The 25-mile flight took 17 minutes and cost $7.50. *Tampa Tribune 7-26-59*

The main operations base of Eastern Air Lines was established in 1934 at Miami's 36th Street Airport. Eastern's 1st president and GM was best known as a top flying ace in World War I—but you got me who he was! Was he. . . ?
  1. **Eddie Rickenbacker**
  2. **Manfred von Richthoven**
  3. **Waldo Pepper**

Rickenbacker. *Highlights of Greater Miami by J. Calvin Mills*

Fly the friendly skies
Southern Air Transport, an airline based in Miami, was—you got me! Was it. . . ?
  1. **The 1st airline to take advantage of price deregulation**
  2. **Run by the CIA**
  3. **The predecessor of UPS**

The airline was part of the CIA's massive operation in south Florida. *Miami by Joan Didion*

June 1, 1937, one of the world's most famous pilots began an around-the-world flight by departing from Miami and flying east on Pan Am's regular route. While over the Pacific on July 2nd, at 1912 GMT, the pilot radioed: "one-half hour fuel and no landfall"—but you got me

who that was! Was it. . . ?
1. **Fred Noonan**
2. **Amelia Earhart**
3. **Charles Lindbergh**

Amelia Earhart. *[thehistorynet.com] and Amelia Earhart by Doris L. Rich*

On May 11, 1996, a ValuJet DC-9 took off from Miami and crashed into the Everglades, tragically killing all 110 on board. Flight 592 was originally scheduled to fly to. . . ?
1. **Atlanta**
2. **Washington**
3. **Newark**

The flight was scheduled to Atlanta. In 1997 ValuJet merged with AirWays and flies under the name AirTran Airways. *Facts on File 8-21-97 and 5-16-96*

On the fly

The 1st commercial airline flight between Havana and Key West in 1929 was the predecessor of the Latin-American operations from Miami of—you got me! Was it. . . ?
1. **TWA**
2. **Pan Am**
3. **Eastern**

Pan American World Airways. *[florida.com]*

On October 18, 1982, Orlando International Airport saw the first-ever landing of—you got me what!
1. **2 supersonic Concordes side by side**
2. **A stealth bomber**
3. **The space shuttle**

2 Concordes landed side by side as part of EPCOT's opening festivities. *Greater Orlando Aviation Authority press release*

During World War II there were 3 air fields around Tampa Bay: MacDill Field (which became MacDill AFB), Drew Field (which became Tampa International Airport), and Henderson Field, which became— you got me! Did it become. . . ?

1. Tampa Stadium
2. Busch Gardens
3. The University of South Florida

Busch Gardens. *Tampa Tribune 10-22-79*

What a long, strange trip: Florida roads

Life in the fast lane
In July 1957 the speed limit posted along the state's highways was 65 mph during the day, 55 at night (trucks: 50 and 45). But you got me what Florida's posted speed limit was prior to 1957! Was it. . . ?
1. 45 mph
2. 55 mph
3. There wasn't one

There wasn't a posted speed limit, but speeds over 60 mph were deemed "reckless driving." *Tampa Tribune 7-20-57*

Hit the road
On Friday, May 9, 1980, a cargo ship, the *Summit Venture,* crashed into a Florida bridge during a thunderstorm, knocking out a chunk of the span and sending cars and a Greyhound bus plunging into the bay. But you got me what bridge! Was it. . . ?
1. The Card Sound Bridge
2. The Seven Mile Bridge
3. The Sunshine Skyway Bridge

The Sunshine Skyway Bridge. A new Skyway was built, and sections of the original now serve as a fishing pier. *Tampa Times 5-9-80*

Pave paradise
As of December 1987, when the final stretch of I–95 opened in Florida, you could at last drive all the way from Miami to the interstate's northern terminus in—you got me! Was it. . . ?
1. Silver Springs, MD
2. Houlton, ME
3. Owego, NY

Houlton, ME, is the northern terminus of I–95; 382.4 miles are in Florida. *Some Kind of Paradise by Mark Derr*

You take the high road
When the AAA Motor Club named the top 10 roads in the nation in 1998, Florida had—you got me how many!
1. 2
2. 3
3. 5

Three. The Florida roads awarded were Bayshore Boulevard in Tampa, the Central Florida Greenway in Orlando, and A1A in Fort Lauderdale. *St. Petersburg Times 5-12-98*

Watch your step
Of the nation's top 3 most dangerous places to be a pedestrian, you got me how many are in the state of Florida! Is it. . . ?
1. 1
2. 2
3. All of them

The top 3 are in Florida: Orlando, Tampa/St. Petersburg, and Miami/Fort Lauderdale. Rounding out the list are Providence, Phoenix, Houston, Atlanta, Los Angeles, Buffalo, NY, and Charlotte, NC. *Surface Transportation Policy Project (1998)*

The very first specialty license plates in the nation were introduced in Florida in 1987 to honor those killed in—you got me! Was it. . . ?
1. Vietnam
2. The space shuttle
3. Drunk-driving accidents

The plate commemorated the astronauts killed in the *Challenger* explosion. Today, about 8% of Florida vehicles have designer tags, the most popular being "Protect the Panther." *St. Petersburg Times 12-29-98*

Florida is one of the nation's most lenient when it comes to driver's license renewals. But you got me how long it's possible to go without being required to take any kind of driver's test. Is it. . . ?
1. 6 years
2. 11 years
3. 18 years

Licenses are renewed every 6 years, with no test required until after the second renewal; you could go 18 years test-free. *New York Times 10-21-98*

One for the road
Carl Fisher, best known as the developer behind Miami Beach, also had a hand in developing the 1st north-south highway in the nation, from Chicago to Miami—but you got me what highway that was! Was it the. . . ?
1. **Fisher Highway**
2. **Dixie Highway**
3. **Miacago Highway**

Dixie Highway. *Who Was Who in Florida by Henry S. Marks*

In November 1909 the *Tampa Daily Times* sponsored a 543-mile endurance car race from Tampa to Jacksonville, and back. Today, that's 8 hours tops—but you got me how long it took in 1909! Was it. . . ?
1. **13 hours**
2. **33 hours**
3. **53 hours**

Fifty-three hours over the sandy, winding trails of the day. *Tampa Times 7-24-65*

After the Labor Day hurricane of 1935 washed out Henry Flagler's Miami to Key West train and the Overseas Highway was built in its place, you got me what became of Henry's tracks! Were they. . . ?
1. **Sunk as artificial reefs**
2. **Used as guardrails**
3. **Sold to the Japanese, who turned them into bullets**

Some of the tracks were put up as guardrails. *St. Petersburg Times 8-2-82*

BONUS Overseas Highway question
You got me how many bridges you drive over on the Overseas Highway from the mainland to Key West! Are there. . . ?
1. **17**
2. **37**
3. **67**

There are 37 bridges, including Florida's longest, the Seven Mile Bridge. *St. Petersburg Times 8-2-82*

After 10 years of construction, the 132.1-mile highway connecting Daytona Beach with the Tampa Bay area opened in March 1965—but you got me what road that is! Is it. . . ?

1. **The Florida Turnpike**
2. **I–95**
3. **I–4**

I–4, through Orlando. *Tampa Tribune-Times 4-18-76*

In November 1924 the longest toll bridge in the world, the Gandy Bridge, cut 24 miles off the trip from Tampa to St. Petersburg and averaged in its 1st year 2,000 cars per day. You got me what the toll for car and driver was in those days! Was it. . . ?

1. **50¢**
2. **$5**
3. **$15**

Fifty cents for car and driver, plus 10¢ for each additional passenger. Today, it's toll-free. *Tampa Tribune 11-20-25*

Beyond belief

In 1935 Robert Ripley of "Believe It or Not" fame drew a cartoon about the bridge that was dedicated in Fort Myers to Thomas Alva Edison not long before the inventor's death. But you got me what was so unbelievable about the Edison Memorial Bridge! Was it. . . ?

1. **It wasn't a bridge at all**
2. **Edison was phobic about bridges**
3. **It was unlighted**

The bridge honoring the inventor of the incandescent electric light was not illuminated. *Tampa Tribune 3-5-61*

King of the road

In 1763 the British constructed King's Road from New Smyrna through St. Augustine and Cow Ford (now Jacksonville), which eventually connected in Georgia with roads going north to Boston and Philadelphia. But you got me which King of England King's Road was named for! Was it. . . ?

1. **George III**
2. **Henry VIII**
3. **Louis XIV**

George III had assumed the throne 3 years before, in 1760 (the same George III we fought in the American Revolution). King's Road is still a street in Jacksonville. *All-Florida Magazine 5-28-55*

In 1883 construction commenced on something that was supposed to be 50 feet wide and extend from Jacksonville to Miami—but you got me what! Was it. . . ?

1. US 1
2. The Intracoastal Waterway
3. The East Coast Railroad

The original Intracoastal Waterway was designed to be 5 feet deep and 50 feet wide. *Florida Inland Navigation District guide map*

Go and play in the traffic

By some accounts, Miami's 1st automobile was a 1901 Locomobile used as a taxi—but you got me how many cars Miami had by 1904! Was it. . . ?

1. 2
2. 10
3. 48

There were 10 cars. *Miami 1909 by Thelma Peters*

BONUS early Miami question

You got me what Miami's 1st speed limit was in 1906. Was it. . . ?

1. No faster than horse trots
2. 8 mph on straightaways, 5 mph at corners
3. 25 mph for cars, 20 for trucks

Eight mph on straightaways, 5 mph at corners. *Miami 1909 by Thelma Peters*

Far out

Mileage markers on the Overseas Highway often serve as addresses. Mile Zero is at the corner of Whitehead and Fleming, in Key West—but you got me where the last one is! Is it. . . ?

1. Key Largo
2. Marathon Key
3. Islamorada

Marker #126 is on Key Largo, just before you get to the mainland. *AAA Tour Book—Florida and Frommer's Florida*

E. P. Dickie of the Tampa Board of Trade is credited with thinking up the odd name of the famous road that opened April 25, 1928—but you got me which one! Is it. . . ?
1. **Alligator Alley**
2. **Tamiami Trail**
3. **Spook Hill**

 The 283.9-mile Tamiami Trail combines the names of the terminus cities of Tampa and Miami. *Tampa Tribune 4-23-72*

SWAMP THING

St. Augustine Alligator Farm and Zoological Park,
circa 1940

Chapter 4

Featured Creatures— Florida Wildlife

A female egret is not an egress: Florida birds

Bye bye, birdie

After 20 years on Fish and Wildlife Service's endangered species list, the last dusky seaside sparrow, a bird named Orange Band, sang his swan song on June 16, 1987, at—you got me where! Was he at. . . ?

1. **The Apalachicola National Forest**
2. **The Canaveral National Seashore**
3. **Walt Disney World**

Walt Disney World. *[theatlantic.com]*

A popular nesting site in Tampa Bay called Rookery Key was terrorized in 1996 by a single animal that in 6 weeks' time ate the eggs and drove off the hundreds of pelicans, egrets, and herons. But you got me what kind of animal could wreak that much havoc! Was it. . . ?

1. **One diamondback rattler**
2. **One wiener dog**
3. **One raccoon**

It was a raccoon. *St. Petersburg Times 5-6-98*

The Mary Kay of birds

In 1931 Hialeah Race Course received from Cuba the first of its trademark flamingoes. The birds were wrapped in newspaper, tied for the flight, and released at Hialeah in the afternoon. But you got me what had happened by the next morning! Was it. . . ?

1. **All their feathers fell out**
2. **They were gone**
3. **They croaked**

They flew away, probably back to Cuba. *Hialeah Race Course Guide Book 1951*

Fashion victim
Around 1900, the beautiful birds, Roseate spoonbills, were nearly entirely killed off for their feathers, which were sold as fans. But you got me how much a spoonbill wing brought in in those days! Was it. . . ?
1. 20¢
2. $2
3. $20

Roseate spoonbill wings fetched $2 per wing, $4 for the whole bird. There are today an estimated 1,000 to 1,200 nesting pairs in Florida. *Tampa Tribune 6-28-98*

Scientists from the South Florida Water Management District have found a new way to invite wading birds to ponds. They put a classic piece of Florida kitsch to good use—but you got me what! Is it. . . ?
1. Lawn jockeys
2. Snow domes
3. Plastic pink flamingoes

Plastic lawn flamingoes, repainted white, and called snowmingoes. *Sounds Like Science (NPR)*

Good egg
The 1st flamingo ever hatched in captivity was in 1937 at—you got me! Was it. . . ?
1. Marineland
2. Cypress Gardens
3. Hialeah Race Course

At Hialeah. *Hialeah Race Course Guide Book (1951)*

Two in the bush
Cormorants and anhingas look alike and are often mistaken for one another, but you got me which is the all black one with a hooked bill! Is it. . . ?
1. Cormorant
2. Anhinga
3. Neither has a hooked bill

Cormorants are all black with hooked bills and hang out at the coast, whereas anhingas have brownish patterned tails, straight bills, and go more for fresh water. *Florida Wildlife Mar/Apr 1980*

The Eagle has landed
Florida claims the 2nd largest resident population of bald eagles (the national symbol since 1782)—but you got me which state has more! Is it. . . ?
  1. Washington
  2. California
  3. Alaska

Alaska, where from 1917 until 1952 the state paid a bounty for killing them. *Florida Birds, National Geographic Jan 1961, and Tampa Tribune-Times 2-12-78*

Birds who talk to Ralph on the big white phone
If you disturb a vulture while he's chowing down on roadkill, he'll probably—you got me what he'll do! Is it. . . ?
  1. Attack! Attack!
  2. Upchuck
  3. Call for reinforcements

Vultures usually vomit, ornithologists say. *St. Petersburg Times 12-16-82*

Along with perhaps the largest surviving stand of mature bald cypress trees, the 11,000 acres of Corkscrew Swamp are home to the country's largest remaining colony of—you got me! Is it. . . ?
  1. Flamingoes
  2. Wood storks
  3. Roseate spoonbills

Wood storks, North America's only native stork. *St. Petersburg Times 4-6-75*

Five states, including Florida, have selected as their official state bird—you got me! Is it the. . . ?
  1. Mockingbird
  2. Bluebird
  3. Cardinal

The mockingbird (*Mimus polyglottos,* meaning "many-tongued mimic") was designated Florida's state bird in 1927. The other states are Arkansas, Mississippi, Tennessee, and Texas. *Florida Handbook 1997–1998*

🐦 BONUS mockingbird question

When a male mockingbird is in the market for a mate, he does something that he doesn't ordinarily do—but you got me what! Is it. . . ?
1. Gets "drunk" on Brazilian peppers
2. Sings at night
3. Flies faster

Males sing at night. *St. Petersburg Times 8-29-98*

Out of Africa

First seen here in 1952, the cattle egret is an Old World species associated with the East African plains—but you got me how they got over here! Was it. . . ?
1. The Spaniards brought them as food
2. They were imported by the pet trade
3. A strong storm blew them here

According to some theories, they rode the high winds of a strong storm across the Atlantic; stowaways on board a freighter is another theory. *At Water's Edge and Florida's Birds by Herbert W. Kale II and David S. Maehr*

A marvelous bird is a pelican; its beak holds more than its belly can

Brown pelicans do something in Florida that the American white pelicans don't—but you got me what! Is it. . . ?
1. Breed
2. Sing
3. Change color

Brown pelicans breed in Florida; the American white winters here but breeds in the northern midwest and Canada. *Florida's Birds by Herbert W. Kale II and David S. Maehr*

If you knew sushi like I know sushi: Florida marine life

Tough customer

One of the denizens in waters around Sanibel, the torpedo ray, has a nasty streak. Mess with him and he just might—you got me! Would he. . . ?
1. Jab fishhooklike barbs into you
2. Zap you with 200-plus volts of electricity
3. Slime you with inky black stuff

Zap you with 200-plus volts of electricity. *The Nature of Things on Sanibel Island by George R. Campbell*

The sharks' teeth that beachcombers find on Manatee, Sarasota, and Charlotte County beaches are most commonly black and about ½ inch long—but you got me how old they are. Are they. . . ?
1. Generally only a few weeks old
2. Usually between 2 and 10 years
3. 7 to 15 million years old

The petrified sharks' teeth are from the Miocene era, 7 to 15 million years ago. Venice Beach is one of the best spots to find them. *Tampa Tribune 7-9-78*

If they'd only hold still long enough

You got me how many pairs of moving parts a crayfish has got! Is it. . . ?
1. 8 pairs
2. 12 pairs
3. 19 pairs

Nineteen pairs (the abdomen's got 6, the thorax has 8, and the head has 5). *Florida Wildlife June 1969*

Old wives' tale

There's an old saying among the Greek sponge divers in Tarpon Springs that sponges cannot be seen by—you got me who! Is it. . . ?
1. A bachelor
2. A blue-eyed man
3. A bowlegged man

The saying is that a blue-eyed man cannot see sponge. *Tampa Tribune-Times 7-11-76*

Biologists in the field use these distinctive marks to tell one manatee from another—but you got me what! Are they. . . ?
  1. Scars from boat propellers
  2. Nose prints
  3. "Freckle" patterns on tails

Prop scars. *St Petersburg Times 1-2-98*

The other white meat
In 1982 a 364-pound tiger shark was reeled in off Hollywood. But you got me what was found in the beast's stomach. Was it. . . ?
  1. A man's leg
  2. An inflatable Shamu pool toy
  3. A pink flamingo lawn ornament

A man's right leg, complete with sock and tennis shoe. Florida averages 16 shark attacks a year. *St. Petersburg Times 9-5-82 and 6-15-99*

Sea turtles, adapting to their ocean habitat, lost the ability to do something that their counterparts on land can do—but you got me what! Is it. . . ?
  1. They can't pull their heads inside their shells
  2. They can't breathe air
  3. They can't walk on land

They lost the ability to retract their heads as their shells became more streamlined. *Sea Turtles: The Watcher's Guide by Timothy O'Keefe*

Beauty and the beast
Christopher Columbus believed these creatures to be mermaids, though "not as beautiful as they are painted." But you got me what! Were they. . . ?
  1. Manatees
  2. Dolphins
  3. Otters

Manatees. *Florida Handbook 1997–1998*

🐾 BONUS manatee question
Manatees eat as much as a tenth of their body weight daily. But you got me how much time your typical sea cow spends chowing down! Is it. . . ?

1. For about an hour 'round midnight
2. About one-fourth of their time
3. They eat 24/7

About one-fourth of the time is spent browsing. *Florida Handbook 1997–1998*

Strong enough for a man, but made for a woman
You got me who sharks sink their teeth into most! Is it. . . ?
   1. Sharks chow down on men much more often
   2. Women get bitten about twice as often
   3. Sharks don't care; they attack women and men in about equal numbers

Men get bitten much more often. According to one report, about 13½ men for every woman. *Tampa Tribune 4-24-78*

You have the right to remain silent
Harassing a manatee while it's feeding, catching 40, or making manatee whoopee can get you a year in the pokey and—you got me what kind of fine! Is it. . . ?
   1. $200
   2. $2,000
   3. $20,000

$20,000. *St Petersburg Times 1-2-98*

Another manatee bonus
You got me what kind of sound a frightened manatee makes! Is it. . . ?
   1. Hissing like a snake
   2. Squeaks and squeals
   3. Not audible to the human ear

They squeak and squeal. *St Petersburg Times 1-2-98*

When taking a dip in the vicinity of a barracuda, it's a good idea to avoid having something on your person—but you got me what! Is it. . . ?
   1. Glittering things
   2. A mullet
   3. Coconut-scented sunscreen

'Cudas are attracted to glittering objects. *St. Petersburg Times 9-4-77*

Chew on this

In Florida, between 1948 and 1995, you got me whether there were more alligator attacks or shark attacks! Were there. . . ?

1. **More gator attacks**
2. **More shark attacks**
3. **Both were the same**

There were 276 shark attacks (6 fatalities), but only 218 gator attacks (with 7 fatalities). That translates: If a shark gets you, you've got a 2% chance of buying the farm, but with a gator the chance is 3.4%. *[flmnh.ufl.edu]*

BONUS man-eater question

You got me which one packs the biggest bite! Is it. . . ?

1. **A great white shark**
2. **An alligator**
3. **Both have the same chomping power**

A great white's bite is about 1,700 pounds per square inch; a 12-foot gator's is about 3,200. *Florida Survival Handbook by Mike Vizcary*

A walk on the wild side

Called *pla duk dam* in its native Thailand and brought here in the '60s, these fish can breathe air and walk on land. But you got me what they are! Are they. . . ?

1. **Walking catfish**
2. **Strolling bass**
3. **Toddling trout**

Walking catfish (*Clarias batrachus*). *Florida Wildlife May 1975*

Badgers? We don't need no stinking badgers: Florida critters

According to one report the ubiquitous nine-banded armadillo 1st came to Florida in 1924—but you got me how he got here! Was it. . . ?

1. **In freight on a slow boat from China**
2. **In a circus truck that overturned, releasing them into the wild**
3. **They swam across the Florida Straits from Cuba**

A circus truck overturned and they escaped into the wild. (Other sources differ.) *Around Lake Okeechobee by Bill and Carol Gregware*

🐾 BONUS armadillo question
Spook an armadillo and you got me what he'll do! Will he. . . ?
1. Play dead
2. Buck like a bucking bronco
3. Withdraw into his shell

When alarmed, armadillos give an upward kick like a bucking bronco. *Tampa Tribune 4-22-78*

Not a creature was stirring
You got me what a Chadwick beach cotton mouse has in common with the pallid beach mouse! Is it. . . ?
1. They both migrated here from Africa
2. They top the list of Florida nuisance pests
3. They're extinct

They're extinct since 1938 and 1946 respectively. According to one report, nearly 17% of Florida's native animals face the danger of extinction. *Forum, The Magazine of the Florida Humanities Council, Spring/Summer 1993*

Brown shag carpet down through the ages
During and before the Ice Age, huge herds of these beasts roamed the Florida woodlands—but you got me what! Were they. . . ?
1. Mastodons
2. Spotted camels
3. Rhinoceroses

Complete skeletons of *Mastodon americanus* have been removed from many sites, including the Itchatucknee River. We also had true elephants that stood 15–16 feet tall. *Florida State Board of Conservation 12-31-40*

Everybody's got something to hide
Since 1974, a subsidiary of Bausch & Lomb has bred and raised for scientific testing these creatures that roam free on Key Lois and Raccoon Key. But you got me what kind of creatures they are! Are they. . . ?
1. Monkeys
2. White Rats
3. Fruit flies

Charles River Laboratories raises monkeys for vaccines and other testing. *Florida Handbook 1997–1998*

Country bears after the jamboree
Of the 104 threatened Florida black bears found dead in 1998, 90 of them were killed by—you got me! Was it. . . ?
1. Cars
2. Hunters
3. Other black bears

A record 90 were roadkill in 1998. The population, once 12 thousand, is today estimated at 1,500 to 3,000. *St. Petersburg Times 1-14-99*

Little black book
You got me which of these creatures associated with Florida is the only one mentioned in the Bible! Is it. . . ?
1. An alligator
2. A flamingo
3. A greyhound

The greyhound. *Proverbs 30:31*

A horse is a horse of course of course
About 25 million years ago during the Miocene Period, herds of unusual horses roamed the Florida prairies—but you got me what was so unusual about them! Was it. . . ?
1. They had horns
2. They were dog-size
3. They were snow white

The dog-size remains of those horses were found in Gilchrist County in the 1930s. *Florida State Board of Conservation 12-31-40*

You've really got a hold on me
Not that you'll be in any condition to count, but if an alligator sank all his teeth into you, that would be—you got me how many! Is it. . . ?
1. 32, same as people
2. 40 to 50
3. 70 to 80

70 to 80. *Guide to Florida Alligator and Crocodile by Robert Anderson*

Go, cat, go
In 1981 the endangered Florida panther was chosen over the alligator, the key deer, and the manatee as the official state animal. But you got me who did the choosing? Was it. . . ?

1. Elementary school children
2. The Florida Legislature
3. Cyrus J. Turling, age 106, the state's oldest native resident

Florida schoolchildren voted for their favorite animal. *Tampa Tribune 11-7-81*

The way you look tonight

At night if you shined your flashlight at an alligator and its eyes looked red—you got me what you could tell by that! Could you tell. . . ?
1. The gator is a baby
2. The gator is an adult male
3. The gator is sleeping

Adult male gators' eyes reflect red; females and immatures look greenish. *Guide to Florida Alligator and Crocodile by Robert Anderson*

BONUS gator question

Gators use only their tails for swimming, with back feet serving as a rudder—but you got me how fast a gator can swim! Is it. . . ?
1. 5 mph
2. 16 mph
3. 30 mph

Gators have been clocked at 14 knots, or 16 mph. *Guide to Florida Alligator and Crocodile by Robert Anderson*

Another gator BONUS

When a gator grunts, you got me what he's trying to say! Is it. . . ?
1. Hello
2. Back off, Jack
3. I could use a little bite

Gators grunt to say hello; they hiss and blow when unhappy. *All-Pets Magazine July 1937*

Get stuffed

In 1965 Britons snapped up 18-inch stuffed baby alligators that were offered at 5 London stores. But you got me how much you could expect to fork over for a gator! Was it. . . ?
1. About 15 cents

2. About $3
3. About $90

Twenty-one shillings, or about $2.94. *AP 7-19-65*

According to the *Memoir* of Escalante Fontaneda, published in Spain around 1575, some creature ranged in considerable herds across central Florida, but you got me what! Was it. . . ?
1. Moose
2. Buffalo
3. Kangaroo

Buffalo. *Tampa Tribune 11-21-54 and Memoir of d'Escalante Fontaneda Respecting Florida*

About 15 miles south of St. Augustine, Rattlesnake Island in the 1980s was one of the last known habitats of one weaselly Florida creature—but you got me what! Was it. . . ?
1. The Florida mongoose
2. The Florida mink
3. The Florida vole

The Florida mink. *Tampa Tribune 10-31-82*

Boarish behavior
Wild hogs, some up to 500 pounds and bigger than bears, are found in many places around the state, including Myakka River State Park near Sarasota—but you got me where they originally came from! Were they. . . ?
1. Driven into Florida by the last Ice Age
2. Descendants of domestic pigs brought by the Spanish
3. They evolved from prehistoric sloths

They descended from domestic pigs brought by the Spanish. *Some Kind of Paradise by Mark Derr*

Around 130,000 years ago, giant creatures 15 to 20 feet tall, 8 feet wide, and weighing 3 to 5 tons were wandering around coastal Florida—but you got me what they were! Were they. . . ?
1. Giant queen conchs
2. Giant ground sloths
3. Giant armadillos

Giant ground sloths. *[www.vas.org]*

We don't just make your snake, we make your snake deadly

Diamondback rattlesnakes are Florida's largest and most dangerous native snake. But you got me if the newborn ones are dangerous! Are they. . . ?

1. Harmless for the 1st few weeks of life
2. Born with venom, but fangless
3. Born loaded and ready for action

They're born loaded with venom and ready for action. *Florida Game and Fresh Water Fish Commission*

Bite me: Florida bugs

I've got you under my skin

When a mosquito puts the pedal to the metal, you got me how fast he's going! Is it. . . ?
1. $\frac{1}{10}$ mph
2. 1 to 1½ mph
3. 3½ to 4 mph

1 to 1½ mph. *[www.science.mcmaster.ca]*

He loves and she loves

Love bugs, a blot on Florida windshields in April/May and again in August/September, hang around highways because they're attracted to—you got me! Is it. . . ?
1. Roadkill
2. Car exhaust
3. Headlights

Love bugs are drawn to highways by the smell of car exhaust exposed to sunlight. The acid in their bodies can ruin car finishes. *[www.sno-bird.com]*

Hey, Mikey, he likes it

In 1967 archivists fished Florida's 4th Constitution (1868), known as the "Carpetbag Constitution," out of the walk-in storage vault in the Capitol and made an unpleasant discovery—but you got me what! Was it. . . ?

1. The ink had disappeared
2. Cockroaches had eaten it
3. Someone had spilled coffee all over it

Roaches ate a baseball-size hole in the document, damaging it beyond repair. Florida has had 6 constitutions. *Tampa Tribune 6-18-67 and St. Petersburg Times 1-29-84*

They're everywhere you want to be

Before control programs kicked in, Sanibel held the world record for mosquitoes. But you got me how many mosquitoes were caught in one light-trap in a single night! Was it. . . ?
1. Nearly 5,000
2. Nearly 30,000
3. Nearly 400,000

Nearly 400,000 in a single trap. *U.S. Fish and Wildlife Service, July 1980*

Itching for a fight

During the Seminole Wars, the U.S. Army commonly suffered the greatest number of casualties from attack by anopheles—but you got me what *anopheles* were! Were they. . . ?
1. A renegade tribe of Creek Indians
2. Mosquitoes
3. Bahamian pirates who plied the Keys

The malaria-carrying mosquito. Malaria was still common here into the 1930s. *Florida Wildlife May/June 1978*

The wingspan of the average adult dragonfly bouncing off your car is about 3 to 5 inches. If you'd been driving here 2 million years ago, you got me how big the dragonflies were! Were they. . . ?
1. The same; dragonflies haven't changed
2. The size of mosquitoes
3. Nearly 3 feet in wingspan

One extinct species had a 3-foot wingspan. *St. Petersburg Times 8-7-82*

Stuck inside of Mobile

These pests 1st entered the country aboard a ship into Mobile, Alabama, in 1918, and sometime in the 1940s underwent a sea change: changing color from black to brownish red and turning

mean. But you got me what they are! Are they. . . ?
1. **Palmetto bugs**
2. **Fire ants**
3. **Killer bees**

Fire ants. *St. Petersburg Times 4-10-77*

✿ BONUS fire ant question
You got me how a fire ant delivers his burning sting! Does he. . . ?
1. **Hang on with his jaws and stick you with his stinger**
2. **Hang on with his sticky feet and bite you**
3. **Relieve himself on you**

Hang on with his jaws and stick you with his stinger. *St. Petersburg Times 4-10-77*

Even educated fleas do it
Queen termites produce eggs at a rate of—you got me! Is it. . . ?
1. **10 to 30 per day**
2. **1,000 to 3,000 per day**
3. **10,000 to 30,000 per day**

10,000 to 30,000 or more per day. *World Book Encyclopedia*

✿ BONUS termite question
Your typical adult mayfly has got a few days or hours to live. But you got me how long your basic termite queen has got in her! Is it. . . ?
1. **One mating cycle (4 months)**
2. **2 years is old**
3. **50 years**

50 years or more. *World Book Encyclopedia*

When you've got 'em, you don't want 'em
Kicking off a summerlong fiasco in the Tampa Bay area, Florida agriculture commissioner Bob Crawford announced on May 29, 1997, that something had been found in a kumquat tree on Hanna Avenue—but you got me what! Was it a. . . ?
1. **Dusky seaside sparrow, believed extinct**
2. **Mediterranean fruit fly**
3. **An Iraqi spy**

 Mediterranean fruit fly. *Department of Agriculture press release 5-29-97*

Chapter 5

Write-Off—Authors in Florida

Hemingway in Florida

You can't tell a book by its cover
Ernest Hemingway's *The Old Man and the Sea* ran in its entirety in a popular magazine in 1952—but you got me what magazine! Was it. . . ?
1. *Playboy*
2. *Life*
3. *Field and Stream*

Life **magazine bought it for $40,000.** *Tampa Tribune 9-13-70*

Hemingway arrived in Florida in 1928. His only Florida-set novel (arguably his worst) was made into a Howard Hawks movie starring Humphrey Bogart and Lauren Bacall. But you got me what it was! Was it. . . ?
1. *To Have and Have Not*
2. *The Big Sleep*
3. *Key Largo*

To Have and Have Not. Florida Handbook 1997–1998 and Leonard Maltin's Movie and Video Guide 1993

O Captain, my Captain
Gregorio Fuentes Betancourt, who skippered Ernest Hemingway's fishing boat *Pilar* for 27 years, was the model for Santiago in—you got me what Hemingway book! Was it. . . ?
1. *The Pearl*
2. *The Old Man and the Sea*
3. *To Have and Have Not*

He was the model for Santiago in *The Old Man and the Sea,* the last of Hemingway's novels published during his lifetime. *Tampa Tribune 6-4-78 and 9-13-70*

The young babe and the sea

Hemingway is said to have first set eyes on his 3rd wife, Martha Gelhorn, when she popped her head into a place where Ernest hung out in Key West. But you got me what place! Was it. . . ?
1. A bar called Sloppy Joe's
2. A restaurant called Eat at Joe's
3. A boxing gym called Punchy Joe's

A bar called Sloppy Joe's. *Florida Handbook 1997–1998*

Other authors in Florida

A posthumous anthology of the work of African-American author and Eatonville native, Zora Neale Hurston (1903–1960), was entitled—you got me! Was it. . . ?
1. *I've Enjoyed About as Much of This as I Can Stand*
2. *You're the Reason Our Kids Are Ugly*
3. *I Love Myself When I Am Laughing and Then Again When I Am Looking Mean and Impressive*

I Love Myself When I Am Laughing and Then Again When I Am Looking Mean and Impressive. Hurston's best known work is *Their Eyes Were Watching God.* (The other 2 choices are country songs by Porter Wagoner and Loretta Lynn respectively.) *Encyclopedia Britannica*

🎬 BONUS Hurston question

In 1973 the author of *The Color Purple* travelled to Fort Pierce to place a headstone on the unmarked grave of Zora Neale Hurston, who died in a welfare home on January 28, 1960. But you got me who that author was! Was she. . . ?
1. Alice Walker
2. Nora Roberts
3. Nikki Giovanni

Alice Walker, who wrote on the cover of Hurston's *Their Eyes Are Watching God:* "There is no book more important to me than this one." *Contemporary Black Biography*

Legend has it that this author's wife, Zelda, began her writing career in the '30s at the famous Don CeSar Hotel, a famous pink resort at the south end of Long Key in St. Pete Beach. But you got me who he was! Was he. . . ?
1. Ernest Hemingway
2. William Faulkner
3. F. Scott Fitzgerald

F. Scott Fitzgerald. Developer Thomas J. Rowe named the resort after his favorite opera hero, Don Cesar de Bazan, from *Maritana*. *Tampa Tribune 9-18-91 and 1-14-78*

Keep off the river of grass
The Florida author who in 1922 founded the Herald Baby Milk Fund for the *Miami Herald*, the 1st nonchurch charity except city welfare, is best known for her 1947 book *The Everglades: River of Grass*. But you got me who she was! Was she. . . ?
1. Marjory Stoneman Douglas
2. Zora Neale Hurston
3. Marjorie Kinnan Rawlings

Marjory Stoneman Douglas (1890–1998), who spearheaded the conservation effort to save the Everglades. In 1981 the Tallahassee headquarters of the Department of Natural Resources was named after her. *St. Petersburg Times 5-15-98*

Big bang
In his 1865 science-fiction novel *From the Earth to the Moon*, Jules Verne told the story of men shot to the moon from a giant cannon, the *Columbiad*, in a Florida town. But you got me what town! Was it. . . ?
1. Jacksonville
2. Cape Canaveral
3. Tampa

Verne launched his moon rocket from Stones Hill on the Alafia River outside "Tampa Town." It's thought that Verne pulled the name off a map. Verne's capsule was 12 feet high, aluminum, carried 3 astronauts, and splashed down in the Pacific just like *Apollo 8*. *Tampa Tribune 7-28-57 and Tampa Tribune-Times 6-24-73*

Poetry in motion
One poet associated with New England composed many of his poems

about snowstorms while wintering in balmy Coconut Grove—but you
got me who that was! Was it. . . ?

1. Carl Sandburg
2. Robert Frost
3. Dylan Thomas

Robert Frost. *Miami, City of the Future by T. D. Allman*

New kid on the block
Tallahassee's most historic home, The Grove (home of Ellen Call Long
[1825–1905], reputedly the 1st white child born in that city and the
one about whom Maurice Thompson wrote his novel *Tallahassee Girl)*,
was built by slave labor in the style of The Hermitage, the Nashville
mansion of the 7th President of the U.S. But you got me who that
was! Was it. . . ?

1. James Monroe
2. Andrew Jackson
3. Zachary Taylor

Andrew "Old Hickory" Jackson. *Tampa Tribune 10-24-71*

I spy with my little eye
John James Audubon explored Florida in 1831–1832 and made
detailed observations of 51 kinds of these, painting all of them. But
you got me what! Were they. . . ?

1. Birds
2. Fish
3. Seashells

**Audubon's *Birds of America* began appearing (in installments) in
1827.** *St. Petersburg Times 4-22-79*

🐾 BONUS Audubon question
When he wasn't painting birds, John James Audubon, noted bird
painter in whose honor the National Audubon Society is named,
engaged in another activity involving his fine feathered friends—but
you got me what! Did he like to. . . ?

1. Shoot them
2. Record their songs
3. Stuff them

Audubon was an avid hunter and sportsman. *St. Petersburg Times 4-22-79*

Local color

Longtime Sarasota resident John D. MacDonald is best known for his Travis McGee mysteries. But you got me what all the titles of those mysteries have in common! Is it. . . ?

1. **They all contain a number**
2. **They all include a color**
3. **They all include a smell**

Color: *The Deep Blue Good-By* (1964), *The Green Ripper* (1979), *The Lonely Silver Rain* (1985), and many others. *Benét's Reader's Encyclopedia and Tampa Times 8-17-77*

⚓ BONUS John D. MacDonald question

MacDonald's novel *The Executioners* was made into a 1962 film starring Gregory Peck and Robert Mitchum—but you got me what it was called! Was it. . . ?

1. *Cape Fear*
2. *Executioner's Song*
3. *A Touch of Evil*

Cape Fear. Independent Movie Database [www.us.imdb.com]

James Jones's powerful first novel about Army life in Honolulu before Pearl Harbor was written while Jones worked on charter fishing boats in the Keys. But you got me what it was! Was it. . . ?

1. *From Here to Eternity*
2. *The Power and the Glory*
3. *The Spy Who Came in from the Cold*

From Here to Eternity. The movie adaptation won 8 Oscars, including one for Frank Sinatra as the ill-fated soldier Maggio. *Tampa Times 8-17-77 and Leonard Maltin's Movie and Video Guide*

Rescue me

After the tugboat *Commodore*, packed with weapons bound from Jacksonville to Cuba, sank off the Florida coast in 1897, this *Red Badge of Courage* author spent 30 hours in a lifeboat before coming ashore on Daytona Beach. But you got me who he was! Was he. . . ?

1. **Hart Crane**
2. **Ichabod Crane**
3. **Stephen Crane**

Stephen Crane wrote about the experience in his short story *The Open Boat. Tampa Tribune and the Tampa Times 11-3-68*

Off the beat track

On October 21, 1969, at St. Anthony's Hospital in St. Petersburg, not even 30 units of Type A positive blood could save this hard-drinking Beat-generation author from gastric hemorrhage and cirrhosis of the liver. But you got me who he was! Was he. . . ?

1. Ernest Hemingway
2. Jack Kerouac
3. Hunter S. Thompson

Author of *On The Road,* Kerouac spent his last 3 years on 10th Ave. North in St. Petersburg living with his 3rd wife and his convalescent mother. Watering hole of choice: The Wild Boar. He died at age 47. *St. Petersburg Times 10-29-78 and Weekly Planet May 28–June 6, 1998*

Get ready to rumble

The Pulitzer prize–winning poet Wallace Stevens, who wrote the words ". . . there is no spring in Florida," could've used a little spring in his step to avoid getting punched in the nose by another famous writer in Florida—but you got me who! Was it. . . ?

1. Ernest Hemingway
2. Marjorie Kinnan Rawlings
3. Tennessee Williams

Hemingway, before his Nobel prize. The Stevens line comes from the poem "Indian River" (1923). *Florida Handbook 1997–1998*

Key West had to pass for a Mississippi Gulf town in the movie version of this playwright's *The Rose Tattoo*. The film was shot right next door to his own house at 1431 Duncan Street. But you got me who that writer was! Was he. . . ?

1. Eugene O'Neill
2. Tennessee Williams
3. Neil Simon

Tennessee Williams (1911–1983). *The Kindness of Strangers by Donald Spoto*

Samuel Langhorne Clemens, better known by his pen name Mark Twain, was born November 30, 1835, in the Missouri town of—you got me! Was it. . . ?

1. Florida
2. Orange
3. Flamingo

Clemens was born in the small town of Florida, Missouri. For many years he wintered in Mandarin, Florida, as the next door neighbor of *Uncle Tom's Cabin* author Harriet Beecher Stowe. *Encyclopedia Britannica and Awesome Almanac by Cima Star and Jean F. Blashfield*

Marjorie Kinnan Rawlings

If you want to call me that, smile
Author Marjorie Kinnan Rawlings was sued for invasion of privacy/libel by one of her neighbors, whom Rawlings described as a "spinster resembling an angry and efficient canary." But you got me what book she got sued for! Was it. . . ?
1. *Cross Creek*
2. *The Sojourner*
3. *The Yearling*

Cross Creek. After an 8-day libel trial at which the *New York Times* stationed a reporter, Rawlings' neighbor Zelma Cason was awarded $1 in damages. *Tampa Morning Tribune 12-16-53, Tampa Tribune 11-2-84, and Invasion of Privacy by Patricia Nassif Acton*

In 1928 Marjorie Kinnan Rawlings left her husband and job in New York and moved to a 74-acre orange grove north of Ocala—but you got me what job she left! Was she a. . . ?
1. Newspaperwoman
2. Stage actress
3. Insurance agent

Marjorie Kinnan Rawlings, who won the Pulitzer prize for *The Yearling*, was a newspaperwoman. *Tampa Tribune 11-18-83*

When country bears attack
In Rawlings' *The Yearling*, the deer is named Flag. But you got me what "the great black outlaw bear with one toe missing" was called! Was he. . . ?
1. Gentle Ben
2. Old Slewfoot
3. Big Al

Old Slewfoot. Tom, the bear who played Old Slewfoot in the 1946 MGM movie *The Yearling,* lived until the late 1970s at the Everglades Wonder Gardens in Bonita Springs. *St. Petersburg Times 12-3-78*

In the movie *Cross Creek*, actress Mary Steenburgen, playing Marjorie Kinnan Rawlings, was told: "You need a hotel? Go see Norman Baskin" (MKR's future husband). But you got me who delivered that line in the film? Was it. . . ?
1. **Rip Torn**
2. **Peter Coyote**
3. **Norman Baskin**

Norman Baskin, MKR's widowed husband, had a bit part. Very unlike Mary Steenburgen, Rawlings is described by her longtime maid Idella Parker as 5'7" and 180 pounds, with a taste for Lucky Strikes and whiskey. *Tampa Tribune 11-18-83 and Idella by Idella Parker with Mary Keating*

Following their October 1941 marriage, Marjorie Kinnan Rawlings and Norman Baskin bought Castle Warden, a big stone hotel in St. Augustine, to live in. But you got me what Castle Warden is today! Is it. . . ?
1. **St. Augustine City College**
2. **Ripley's Believe It or Not Museum**
3. **A pet hotel**

 Ripley's Believe It or Not Museum. *Idella by Idella Parker with Mary Keating*

Chapter 6

We Know Where You Live—Florida Places

If you lived here, you'd be home by now:
Florida counties

Of all the counties in the entire nation, which had the highest number of foreign-born residents?
1. Dade
2. Brevard
3. Manhattan

45.1% of Dade County residents are foreign-born: the highest percent in the nation. As cities go, Hialeah's 70.4% beats Miami's 59.7%.
Florida Handbook 1997–1998

You got me how many miles of Atlantic Ocean beachfront have been set aside in Brevard County, where your dog can legally romp in the surf! Is it. . . ?
1. 0
2. Only 3
3. Dogs are legal on every beach

There's no beach in Brevard County where dogs are allowed. *The Florida Dog Lover's Companion by Sally Deneen and Robert McClure*

When the 1st Federal census was taken of Hillsborough County in 1840—you got me how many civilians lived there! Was it. . . ?
1. 96
2. 960
3. 9,600

Ninety-six. Only 4 Latin names appeared as heads of families in the record. *Tampa Town 1824–1886 by Anthony P. Pizzo*

A HOME

OF OUR OWN

Exterior and interior view of the Guerdon Great Lakes trailer, manufactured in Lake City, 1960s

Fits the bill

A county created by the Territorial Council the day after Christmas 1827 was named in honor of the 1st U.S. Secretary of the Treasury (the guy pictured on a ten spot)—but you got me who that was! Was it. . . ?

1. Andrew Jackson
2. Aaron Burr
3. Alexander Hamilton

Hamilton County was named for Alexander Hamilton. *Tampa Tribune 3-21-54*

Water, water, everywhere

With its 7 rivers, Citrus County boasts the nation's largest herd of East Indian—you got me! Are they East Indian. . . ?

1. Manatees
2. Elephants
3. Water buffalo

Manatees. *Florida Heritage Magazine Fall 1996*

Florida today has 67 counties—but you got me how many counties there were in 1821 when the Territory of Florida was organized! Was it. . . ?

1. 2
2. 4
3. 7

St. Johns County (formerly East Florida) and Escambia County (formerly West Florida). By the 1st census in 1830, there were 17. *The Southern Genealogists' Exchange Quarterly 1968*

Hendry County (the Florida county with the highest per-capita income) was named for Francis Asbury Hendry, the cattle king of south Florida. The county seat LaBelle was named for—you got me! Was it named for. . . ?

1. His daughters Laura and Belle
2. The horse he rode into the Battle of Olustee
3. His ex-wife, who got the whole town in the divorce settlement

His daughters. *St. Petersburg Times 8-14-77*

On the town

I hate it when that happens
If you'd been "beaching it" on the island of Passage Key the night of October 25–26, 1921, you could've seen a once-in-a-lifetime sight—but you got me what! Was it. . . ?
1. A tidal wave that swallowed the whole island
2. A 250-foot freighter reappearing after 22 years lost in the Bermuda Triangle
3. The only known sighting of Passy, a Loch Ness Monster–like sea creature

It disappeared under a tidal wave. *Boone's Florida Historical Markers and Sites by Floyd E. Boone*

Mayors not named McCheese
The town of Moore Haven in Glades County has the distinction of being the 1st town in the U.S. to have a mayor who was—you got me! Was it. . . ?
1. A socialist
2. A woman
3. A minor under the legal age of 18

Moore Haven had America's 1st woman mayor. *Know Florida (State of Florida)*

Fun city
The city of Venice, Florida, boasts the only one of its kind in the world for professional clowns. But you got me what! Is it. . . ?
1. School
2. Shoe factory producing clown shoes
3. Retirement home

Clown School. In 1968 in Venice, Irvin Feld, producer of the Ringling Bros. and Barnum & Bailey Circus, convened the 1st class. *St. Petersburg Times 11-24-74 and Florida Handbook 1997–1998*

In Fernandina Beach, the Palace, established in 1903 by a German family, claims to be Florida's oldest one in continuous existence at the same location. But you got me what!
1. A slaughterhouse
2. A saloon
3. A movie theater

The saloon is located in Fernandina's Centre Street Historic District.
Tampa Tribune 5-7-78

Sunny-side up
You got me which one of these is on the Gulf side of the state! Is it. . . ?
1. The First Coast
2. The Gold Coast
3. The Suncoast

The Suncoast is generally from Citrus to Collier Counties on the Gulf side. The Gold Coast is the Palm Beach–Miami area, and the First Coast is northeastern Florida. *Florida Handbook 1997–1998*

If you can't say something nice
Best known for his novels *The Red Badge of Courage* and *Maggie: A Girl of the Streets*, Stephen Crane described one Florida city as "soiled pasteboard that some lunatic babies have been playing with." But you got me what city! Was it. . . ?
1. Pensacola
2. Miami
3. Jacksonville

Jacksonville. *Tampa Tribune and the Tampa Times 11-3-68*

Shiver me timbers
One of the most famous ships in U.S. naval history, the *Constitution (Old Ironsides)* was completed in 1797. When she was rebuilt early in the 20th century, Pensacola sent an important contribution—but you got me what! Was it. . . ?
1. The oak timbers
2. The people of Pensacola privately funded the refitting
3. Her captain came from Pensacola

The oak that went into her reconstruction came from what is the Live Oak Reservation. The timbers were surplus oak stored in Commodore's Pond at the Pensacola Navy Yard. *Stories of Old Pensacola by Celia Myrover Robinson*

In the 20-year stretch from 1915 to 1935, you got me how many hotels were built in Miami Beach! Was it. . . ?
1. 22
2. 52
3. 92

Ninety-two. *Florida Construction and Real Estate Development December 1936*

Not a Paul Newman product

In 1931 Arcadia became the 1st town where a certain meat was processed and sold—but you got me what! Was it. . . ?
1. Gator
2. Rattlesnake
3. Armadillo

Rattlesnake. During the Depression, a Tampa rattlesnake-canning out-fit paid $1 for each rattler dug up by the WPA workers clearing land for MacDill Air Force Base. *Florida Handbook 1997–1998 and Tampa Tribune 6-23-84*

Florida's pioneer resort city was—you got me! Was it. . . ?
1. Enterprise
2. New Smyrna
3. Daytona Beach

During the last half of the 19th century, the town of Enterprise, on the St. Johns River, became a mecca for northerners. *Tampa Tribune 1-16-77*

You can't get there from here

To get to this place in 1880, you had to go by way of Jacksonville, take the steamer for Sanford, and connect with the steamer for Rockledge Landing. From there a carriage would take you across to Indian River, where you would catch the mailboat that runs from Rockledge to Eau Gallie to St. Lucie, and finally to—you got me! Is it. . . ?
1. Lake Worth
2. Pensacola
3. Tampa

Lake Worth, population in 1880 of over 100. *Tampa Tribune 3-14-54*

In 1927 at Daytona Beach was the 1st time ever that a car—you got me! Was it. . . ?
1. Topped 200 mph
2. Made a right on red
3. Had air conditioning

On March 29, 1927, the 1st car went over 200 mph. *Florida Handbook 1997–1998*

Dirt cheap
During the Florida land boom of the 1920s, D. P. Davis sold 300 lots for $1.68 million in less than 2 days for his Davis Islands subdivision in Tampa—but you got me what was noteworthy about those lots! Was it. . . ?
1. Davis didn't own them
2. They were underwater
3. They were underground

The lots were largely underwater at the time he sold them. *Florida Heritage Magazine, Winter 1998 [www.dos.state.fl.us]*

Near Key Largo stands a rock named for the pirate who escaped from a shipwrecked slaver and sailed off the coast of Florida with Blackbeard aboard the *Queen Anne's Revenge*—but you got me who that pirate was! Was he. . . ?
1. Black Caesar
2. Black Antony
3. Black Brutus

Black Caesar's Rock is north of Key Largo. *Who Was Who in Florida by Henry S. Marks*

Knock wood
The reputed largest wooden structure in the world is located near Clearwater—but you got me what it is! Is it a. . . ?
1. Bridge
2. Hotel
3. Hangar

It's the Belleview Mido Resort Hotel. *Florida Handbook 1997–1998*

According to 1997 figures, San Francisco and a Connecticut metropolitan area ranked highest in the nation in per capital income—but you got me what area came in right behind them! Was it. . . ?
1. Tampa Bay
2. West Palm Beach–Boca Raton
3. Sarasota

West Palm Beach–Boca Raton. Palm Beach is the stat's wealthiest county, and Hamilton, the poorest. *The Florida Personal Income Handbook 1999 and Tampa Tribune 6-27-99*

The Mark of Zora
The 1st self-governed, African-American city in the nation was incorporated in 1886 and was the birthplace of author Zora Neale Hurston—but you got me what town that was! Was it. . . ?
1. Eatonville
2. Lippincott
3. Mayberry

Eatonville. *Contemporary Black Biography*

On April 23, 1982, Key West mayor Dennis Wardlow, in response to a border crackdown around the Keys, seceded from the U.S. and declared Key West an independent country—but you got me what he called it! Was it. . . ?
1. The Conch Republic
2. Margaritaville
3. The United Keys of the Caribbean

The Conch Republic. *[www.conchrepublic.com]*

One Florida spot takes its name from the home province in northern Spain of its 1st permanent resident—but you got me what spot! Is it. . . ?
1. Key Biscayne
2. Islamorada
3. St. Augustine

Key Biscayne takes its name from Don Pedro the Biscayan, Keeper of the Swans at the Spanish Court, who hailed from Biscaya in the Basque country. *Florida Wildlife May 1973*

Big chill
After some bad freezes around the turn of the century, town fathers in one Florida municipality briefly changed its name to Lakemont, fearing charges of false advertising—but you got me what town that was! Was it. . . ?
1. 92 in the Shade
2. Frostproof
3. Warm Egg

Frostproof in southern Polk County, where there have been many freezes over the years. *Tampa Tribune 1-15-81*

During the British occupation of Florida, the largest single influx of settlers were the 1,510 colonists (among them Peloponnesians, Italians, and Minorcans) brought over by Scottish physician Andrew Turnbull to work the fields at what is today—you got me! Is it. . . ?
1. New Smyrna
2. Homestead
3. Dunedin

New Smyrna, south of St. Augustine. *The 1763 Spanish Census of Florida*

Clean sweep
The town that gave America the whisk for whisk brooms and the wood for pencils was once the largest city on Florida's west coast. But you got me what town that was! Was it. . . ?
1. Cedar Key
2. Fort Myers
3. Sarasota

Cedar Key. *Tampa Morning Tribune 7-24-51 and St. Petersburg Times 4-9-78*

During the Spanish-American War, newspaperman Richard Harding Davis of the Hearst papers referred to this Florida city as "a squalid, sand-blighted city." But you got me what city that was! Was it. . . ?
1. Tampa
2. Miami
3. Key West

He was talking about Tampa. *Some Kind of Paradise by Mark Derr*

You got me which one of these is a real town in Jackson County! Is it. . . ?
1. One Egg
2. Two Egg
3. Dozen Eggs

Two Egg, along SR 69 near the Alabama line. *Tampa Tribune 6-19-77*

For the laborers at work building his grand Royal Poinciana Hotel, Henry Flagler had a company town built on a damp, undesirable 200-acre plot of land. But you got me what that land is today! Is it. . . ?
1. **West Palm Beach**
2. **Miami Beach**
3. **Jupiter**

West Palm Beach. The Royal Poinciana opened in 1894 with 540 rooms and 17 guests. *Some Kind of Paradise by Mark Derr*

Clowns to the left of me, jokers to the right
From the 1920s until 1956, when the Greatest Show on Earth announced the end of its days as a tented circus, one Florida city served as the circus' winter quarters. But you got me what city! Was it. . . ?
1. **Fort Myers**
2. **Sarasota**
3. **Ocala**

John Ringling announced his choice of Sarasota as the winter quarters of the Ringling Bros. and Barnum & Bailey Circus on March 23, 1927. *The Story of Sarasota by Karl H. Grismer*

An American tragedy
This African-American community a few miles from Cedar Key was the scene of a horrific rampage that began New Year's Day 1923, when a mob of whites torched homes and killed or ran off the residents. The name of that town was. . . ?
1. **Rosewood**
2. **Ford**
3. **Winfield**

When it was over, only 1 home was left standing in Rosewood. *Gainesville Sun 10-17-98*

Right next to the maddening crowd
From the 1971 opening of Disney World until the end of the '80s, you got me what happened to the population of nearby Kissimmee! Did it. . . ?
1. **Hold pretty steady**
2. **Double**
3. **Quadruple**

Kissimmee's population went from 7,500 to 15,000 in 1980, and then doubled again during the '80s. *City of Kissimmee/City Information [www.phoenixat.com]*

In 1885 the doctors of the American Medical Association announced that they considered St. Petersburg/Pinellas Point—you got me! Did they say it was. . . ?
1. The yellow fever capital of America
2. The healthiest place in America
3. The unhealthiest place in America

The healthiest is what they said. *St. Petersburg Times 1-5-98*

"Tampa is more wicked than Gay Paris"
—Judge Horace C. Gordon (1910)

Cigar city
In Tampa's historic Ybor City, about the same time that the cigar industry was cranking up, the city's 1st one of these parlors was opened by Manuel Súarez—but you got me what kind of parlor! Was it. . . ?
1. Beauty
2. Tanning
3. Bolita

Súarez, aka "El Gallego," introduced *bolita,* literally "little ball," an early numbers racket or lottery in the 1880s. Controlled by vice king-pin Charlie Wall into the late 1930s, bolita put a lot of money into the pockets of corrupt civic leaders. Wall was murdered in bed 4-18-55. *The Immigrant World of Ybor City by Gary R. Mormino and George E. Pozetta and Tampa Tribune 9-25-94 and 4-18-55*

Does that include the "All I got was this lousy T-shirt" souvenir?
In 1956 Chamber of Commerce officials estimated that the average convention-goer in Tampa dropped an average of—you got me! Was it. . . ?
1. $24 a day
2. $54 a day
3. $84 a day

$24. *Tampa Times 11-15-56*

Sometimes a cigar is just a cigar

By 1900, cigar workers in Ybor City made more than 100 million cigars by hand per year. But you got me what percentage of Tampa's workforce was employed in the cigar business! Was it. . . ?

1. About 10%
2. About 25%
3. About 75%

About 75% of the city's employed persons were cigar workers. *St. Petersburg Times 6-21-87*

BONUS cigar question

Tampa's 1st cigars were rolled by—you got me who! Was it. . . ?

1. A Cuban slave woman
2. A Caloosa Indian
3. An Italian pastry maker

Count Odet Philippe bought a slave woman in Havana and had her rolling Tampa's 1st cigars in his Oyster Saloon. The count was a great-nephew of French king Louis XVI. *Tampa Town 1824–1886 by Anthony P. Pizzo*

According to the 1860 census, Tampa's richest man was worth—you got me! Was it. . . ?

1. $6,250
2. $62,500
3. $625,000

John Darling was worth $62,500; by 1869, after the Civil War, $125. *Tampa Tribune 9-25-94*

Vote early, vote often

Besides the National Guard being called out to keep order, the 1935 mayoral race in Tampa was noteworthy because—you got me! Was it because. . . ?

1. Tampa's 1st woman mayor was elected
2. There were 3,000 more votes cast than voters
3. A big dog named Tiny was elected mayor

There were 3,000 more votes than voters. Tampa (in those days known as the "Hellhole of the Gulf Coast") was plagued with organized crime and political corruption. *St. Petersburg Times 6-21-87*

A *Tampa Tribune* publicity stunt dating from 1904, Tampa's annual Gasparilla festival honors José Gaspar, who was a—you got me! Was he . . . ?

1. **A Cuban newspaperman**
2. **A pirate**
3. **Tampa's founding father**

Gaspar is said to be a pirate from the early 1800s. *Some Kind of Paradise by Mark Derr*

BONUS excuse-for-a-party question

During the Guavaween celebration held in Ybor City around Halloween, the parade of outrageous floats and uninhibited marchers is known as—you got me! Is it. . . ?

1. **Mardi Guava**
2. **The Mama Guava Stumble**
3. **Carnival of Heroes**

> **The Mama Guava Stumble is adult entertainment and not for the easily offended.** *Florida Weekends by Robert Tolf and Russell Buchan*

A SMORGASBORD OF VICE

Top: Miami city councilors demolishing Carter's
gambling house, 1940
Above: Polk County officers dump 650 gallons of
illicit moonshine, 1956

Chapter 7

Bad Boys, Bad Boys, Whatcha Gonna Do— Florida Crime and Punishment

Crimes and misdemeanors

Take the money and run

On January 8, 1997, a Brinks armored truck crashed and spilled money onto a Miami street, and residents scooped up about $500,000 in cash and another $149,000 in food stamps. People had until January 11 to turn in the money they'd picked up. But you got me how many people turned money in before the amnesty expired! Was it. . . ?

1. 2
2. 222
3. 2,222

Two people turned in a total of $20.38. *Facts on File 1-6-97*

On July 15, 1997, at the only single-family residence on Ocean Drive in South Beach, a man was shot dead on his front steps—but you got me who he was! Was he. . . ?

1. Gianni Versace
2. Andrew Cunanan
3. Bob Monkhouse

Fashion designer Gianni Versace was murdered by Andrew Cunanan. Cunanan later took his own life on a houseboat at 5250 Collins Ave. *[time.com], Sun-Sentinel (Fort Lauderdale), and [herald.com] (Miami Herald)*

Trigger happy

Legendary gunfighter John Wesley Hardin (1853–1895) claimed that he only killed in self-defense—by some accounts, as many as 42 times. Texas Ranger John B. Armstrong and a posse finally snagged him in Pensacola, where he was working as—you got me! Was he a. . . ?

1. Mortician
2. Logger
3. Gun dealer

Logger. *[www.thehistorynet.com] and The People's Almanac #2 by David Wallechinsky and Irving Wallace*

Going my way

Airline hijacking kicked off in the U.S. in 1961. But you got me what year saw the greatest number of "successful" hijackings to Cuba! Was it. . . ?

1. 1961
2. 1969
3. 1979

In 1969, 33 planes were diverted to Cuba. *Tampa Tribune 8-18-80*

Old Joe was found dead of a gunshot wound at the bottom of Wakulla Springs in 1966. A $5,000 reward was posted, but the culprit was never found. Old Joe was—you got me! Was he. . . ?

1. The last of the barefoot mailmen
2. A legendary alligator
3. The 77-year old National Audubon Society president who opposed development around Wakulla

A legendary alligator reputedly (but unlikely) over 200 years old. *UPI 8-4-66 and 8-9-66*

Communication breakdown

To protest the scrambling of cable TV signals, satellite dish dealer John R. MacDougall of Ocala illegally interrupted HBO's transmission of *The Falcon and The Snowman* on April 27, 1986, with a 4½ minute message of his own that stated, "Goodevening HBO from Captain . . . " —who? You got me!

1. Captain America
2. Captain Cable
3. Captain Midnight

The full message was: "Goodevening HBO from Captain Midnight/ $12.95-month? No Way!" (Showtime–Movie Channel Beware!) *Tampa Tribune 7-23-86*

An offer he couldn't refuse

One Tampa native was a high Mafia mogul who ruled gambling interests in Batista's Cuba before Castro ran him out. But you got me who he was! Was he. . . ?

1. Santo Trafficante
2. Albert Anatasia
3. Annello "Little Lamb" Della Croce

Santo Trafficante, who was never convicted of any crime. *UPI 10-16-63*

🏝️ BONUS Trafficante question

Tampa mob lawyer Sam Ragano claimed that he carried a message from union boss Jimmy Hoffa asking alleged Tampa mobster Santo Trafficante to whack someone. But you got me who Hoffa wanted Trafficante to have killed! Was it. . . ?

1. Albert Einstein
2. Frank Sinatra
3. President Kennedy

In his book, *Mob Lawyer,* Ragano said Hoffa wanted JFK assassinated. Ragano claimed that while strolling on Bayshore Boulevard in Tampa, Trafficante told him that the Kennedy assassination was a mob hit. Ragano died in 1998. *St. Petersburg Times 5-14-98*

Set me free why don't you, baby

Of all the crimes for which the 1,251 prisoners were sentenced to Florida prisons in 1941, the top 3 were breaking and entering, grand larceny, and car theft. But you got me what the average sentence of prisoners was! Was it. . . ?

1. About 4 years
2. About 12 years
3. About 20 years

Excluding those sentenced to life terms and death, 4.404 years was average. Ten were convicted of adultery, and 9 for "crime against nature." The most common trade of prisoners: farmer. Religion: Baptist. *27th Biennial Report of the Prison Division of the*

Department of Agriculture of the State of Florida for the Years
1941–1942

You got me what the five Watergate burglars, as well as ex-CIA agent
E. Howard Hunt, did at Eglin Air Force Base! Was it. . . ?
   1. **Plan the break-in of the Democratic National Committee**
      headquarters
   2. **Hide out after the burglary**
   3. **Serve prison sentences**

They were inmates at the Eglin Federal Prison, a minimum-security
"country-club prison." *Tampa Tribune-Times 5-16-76*

🦚 BONUS burglars question

On August 14, 1974, less than a week after President Nixon's resigna-
tion, 3 convicted Watergate burglars announced plans to back a housing development in Polk County—but you got me what the proposed
development was to be called! Was it. . . ?
   1. **Watergate Hills**
   2. **Nixon Palms**
   3. **Tricky Tract**

Watergate Hills. Plumbers Virgilio Gonzalez, Bernard Barker, and
Eugenio Martinez, whose notoriety was intended to pull in curiosity
seekers, later withdrew from the real-estate deal. *Tampa Times 8-28-74*

Smokey and the gangster who dominated organized
crime in Chicago from 1925 to 1931

The 180-acre Burt Reynolds Ranch in Jupiter was once the hideaway
of a famous gangster—but you got me who! Was it. . . ?
   1. **Meyer Lansky**
   2. **Al Capone**
   3. **Bugsy Siegel**

Al Capone. Following Reynolds' 1996 bankruptcy, the ranch was put
on the market. *Current Biography 1973 and [www.the ledger.com]*

Giant sucking sound

In 1990 members of the rap group 2 Live Crew were arrested after a
performance at a Hollywood, FL, nightclub for violating state obscenity laws (a Florida district-court judge had ruled their album
obscene)—but you got me what album that was! Was it. . . ?

1. *As Nasty as They Wanna Be*
2. *In a Metal Mood*
3. *2 Live Crew Sings the Cole Porter Songbook*

As Nasty as They Wanna Be. Band members were acquitted of obscenity charges in Fort Lauderdale, October 1991. The album ended up selling over 3 million copies. *Facts on File 10-26-90 and Who Can It Be Now? by Peter T. Fornatale and Frank R. Scatoni*

I don't know what's wrong with these kids today
In the decade 1985–1995, the rate of violent crime in Florida by kids aged 10–17 was—you got me! Was it. . . ?
1. 20% lower than the U.S. average
2. Exactly the national average
3. 60% higher than the average

60% higher. The juvie arrest rate jumped 68% in those years. *St. Petersburg Times 5-5-98*

But yes, Virginia, there is a Santa Claus
In 1956 a Hillsborough County (Tampa and environs) grand jury returned a finding that there was no such thing as—you got me! Was it. . . ?
1. Political corruption
2. The Mafia
3. Dirty cops

A national or Tampa Mafia. That's what the grand jury said. *UPI 10-16-63*

In a celebrated 1968 case, Emory student Barbara Jane Mackle, daughter of a prominent Coral Gables family, was kidnapped and ransomed for $500,000 by escaped convict Gary Krist and Ruth Eisemann Schier. When the FBI found her, the 20-year-old had spent about 80 hours in her "prison"—but you got me where Mackle was held! Was she. . . ?
1. Buried underground
2. In the reptile house of the Atlanta Zoo
3. In a dryer at a laundromat

On 12-17-68 she was buried in a fiberglass-and-plywood box under 18 inches of dirt in a forest in Gwinnett County, northeast of Atlanta. *Time Capsule 1968 and 83 Hours Till Dawn by Gene Miller with Barbara Jane Mackle*

Money the old-fashioned way

Al Capone, the boss who dominated Chicago's organized crime and in 1928 purchased a home on the north end of exclusive Palm Island (between Miami and Miami Beach), was nicknamed—you got me! Was he known as. . . ?
1. Babyface
2. Scarface
3. Pretty Boy

Scarface Al Capone picked up the scar on his left cheek during a youthful knife or razor fight. *Who Was Who in Florida by Henry S. Marks and Encyclopedia Britannica*

Snow job

In 1989 U.S. troops rousted this strongman from the Vatican Embassy in Panama City and sentenced him in Miami to 40 years for aiding Colombian drug smugglers—but you got me who he is! Is he. . . ?
1. Manuel Noriega
2. William Paca
3. Button Gwinnett

Noriega currently resides in a "well-equipped suite" at Metropolitan Correction Center in Miami, having resisted efforts to get shipped off to the maximum-security federal prison at Marion, IL. (Choices #2 and #3 are signers of the Declaration of Independence.) *St. Petersburg Times 1-16-93 and Facts on File 11-25-93*

BONUS Noriega question

On March 20, 1992, Noriega's wife, Felicidad, was arrested in Miami for shoplifting something—but you got me what! Was it. . . ?
1. A picture of dogs playing poker
2. Car floor mats
3. Buttons

Mrs. Noriega was picked up for ripping $305 worth of buttons off designer dresses at Burdine's. *Facts on File 3-26-92*

On second thought

Nicaraguan Justo Ricardo Somarriba, illegally in the U.S., was at first denied political asylum, but the INS reversed themselves and let him in after—you got me! Was it after. . . ?
1. He was awarded the Nobel prize for Literature
2. He won the Florida Lottery
3. He testified as chief witness against Manuel Noriega

Somarriba won half of the $10.6 million Florida lottery on April 29, 1989. *Facts on File 5-5-89*

Love thy neighbor

On July 16, 1991, Florida couple Alfred Stephens and Janet Paddock were arrested on a felony charge after making whoopee . . . you got me where! Were they. . . ?
1. In the stands during a Marlins home game
2. Inside his apartment
3. In the restroom on a U.S. Airways flight

They were indoors, in Stephens' apartment. A neighbor videotaped them through the apartment window, claiming that the couple was visible from outdoors. The felony charges were later dropped. *Facts on File 8-29-91*

Days after escaping from a Colorado jail (which he did by dropping 40 pounds and squeezing through a hole in the ceiling; his favorite book was *Papillon*), this former Boy Scout, law student, and crisis-hotline worker snuck into a Chi Omega sorority house at Florida State University and brutally murdered 2 St. Petersburg women. Was he. . . ?
1. Jeffrey Dahmer
2. Ted Bundy
3. Albert DeSalvo

Ted Bundy was convicted of the murders, as well as the kidnapping and murder of 12-year-old Kimberly Leach of Lake City. Before he was put to death at dawn on January 24, 1989, Bundy confessed to at least 16 other murders. Demonstrators outside the prison chanted "Chi-O, Chi-O, it's off to Hell you go." *St. Petersburg Times 1-16-78 and 10-1-78, Tampa Times 9-12-80, and Facts on File 1-27-89*

The gang's all here

John Ashley and the notorious Ashley Gang (12 murders and a bunch of robbed banks from 1911 to 1924, when they were gunned down) were the subject of the Hollywood box-office stinker *Big John and Little Laura*. But you got me what teen idol starred as the gang leader! Was it. . . ?

1. Ed "Kooky" Burns
2. Fabian
3. Elvis

Fabian. Karen Black did a turn as his gun moll Laura Upthegrove, self-proclaimed Queen of the Everglades. The real Laura Upthegrove ended it all by drinking disinfectant. *Tampa Times 7-30-82 and The Notorious Ashley Gang by Hix C. Stuart*

Oh give me a home where Buffalo Bob roams

On July 26, 1991, this children's TV host was picked up for indecency in an adult movie theater by Sarasota undercover police—but you got me who he is! Is he. . . ?

1. Captain Kangaroo
2. Pee-wee Herman
3. Barney

Paul Reubens, aka Pee-wee Herman. *Facts on File 8-1-91*

You killed her so completely that we thank you very sweetly

Churchgoing 63-year-old "Mrs. T. C. Blackburn" rented the Bradford house on Lake Weir in Oklawaha in 1934. On January 16, 1935, FBI agents pumped nearly 2,000 rounds into the house during the longest gun battle in FBI annals: 4 hours. But you got me who "Mrs. Blackburn" was really! Was she. . . ?

1. Bonnie Parker
2. Lizzie Borden
3. Ma Barker

Arizona Donnie Clark, alias Ma Barker. *St. Petersburg Times 5-9-83*

Nine-tenths of the law

Possession of *Uniola paniculata* is unlawful, and possession is prima facie evidence of violation. But you got me what it is! Is it. . . ?

1. An endangered oyster
2. A banned strain of California orange
3. A type of grass

A protected type of beach and shore grass commonly known as sea oats. It's also against the law to take *Coccolobis uvifera,* aka sea grapes. *Florida Law 370.041*

According to the Tuskegee Institute's annual report of lynchings in the U.S., you got me how many lynchings there were in Florida in 1929! Were there. . . ?
1. 0
2. 4
3. 10

Florida occupied the shameful top position among the states in the number of lynchings. There were 4 in Florida, 3 in Texas, 1 in Kentucky, 1 in Mississippi, and 1 in Tennessee (7 were African-Americans, 3 were whites). *Tampa Tribune 1-1-30*

On products, like canned goods, that were turned out by Florida prisoners, there was a trademarked brand name on the label—but you got me what it was! Was it. . . ?
1. Betty Cracker brand
2. Dee Cee brand
3. Camp Raiford brand

Dee Cee. Never sold on the open market, prison goods were distributed to other state institutions like mental hospitals. *Tampa Tribune 11-28-58*

Thank you sir, may I have another
In the mid-1800s, sheriffs got to charge additional fees for almost everything they did in the course of doing their job. But you got me how much a sheriff charged for whipping a prisoner! Was it. . . ?
1. 2 bits
2. $2
3. $12

$2; and 50¢ every time they put a man in irons or took him out. *Tampa Daily Times 6-13-53*

🪝 BONUS cost-of-crime question

In 1846 Gadsden County billed the state capital for carrying out 3 executions. Delivering the men to the place of execution cost $2; the coffins ran $6 apiece. But you got me what the gallows cost! Was it. . . ?

1. $25
2. $75
3. $125

$25, including the trap door. The 3 men were sentenced to hang for stealing slaves. *Tampa Daily Times 6-13-53*

D'oh!

In 1997 former armored-car driver Philip Noel Johnson pulled off the nation's largest armored-car robbery: $18.8 million. But you got me where he did it! Was he in. . . ?

1. Miami
2. Orlando
3. Jacksonville

Johnson ripped the money off from an armored car vault in Jacksonville. The loot was eventually recovered from a storage unit in Mountain Home, NC. He successfully escaped to Mexico but then was caught when he crossed back into the U.S. *St. Petersburg Times 9-19-97*

Designated driver

In December 1963 Florida Highway Patrol troopers pulled over an Austin-Healey sports car on I–4 near Lakeland. In the passenger seat was a man named Bob Slover. But you got me what was so unusual about the driver! Was it that. . . ?

1. He was blind
2. He was an 8-year-old
3. He was a chimp

Animal trainer Bob Slover let Cappy, the chimpanzee, drive. The charges were dismissed when Justice of the Peace Marion Hendry failed to find any law on the books saying that chimps couldn't drive cars. *Tampa Tribune 7-5-82*

Smoke 'em if you got 'em: Florida execution

Execution is everything

From 1923 to 1999, one 3-legged, oak electric chair was Florida's only capital-punishment device—but you got me the name by which it was affectionately known! Was it. . . ?

1. Old Reliable
2. Old Bailey
3. Old Sparky

Old Sparky. *"All Things Considered" (NPR) 4-8-97*

You're outta here

On March 30, 1998, Florida did something that it hadn't done since 1848—but you got me what! Was it. . . ?

1. Adopt a new constitution
2. Execute a woman
3. Impeach her governor

Judias Buenoano, the Black Widow, was put to death in Starke, the 42nd in the state since 1976; in 1848 a slave named Celia was hanged for murdering (or as an accessory) the master. *Facts on File 4-2-98*

Discipline pre–Dr. Spock

In the early 1920s electrocution replaced hanging as Florida's method of execution—but you got me what's the youngest age of someone sent to the chair! Is it. . . ?

1. 16
2. 18
3. 21

In the years 1927 and 1941, a total of three 16-year-olds were executed by electrocution. *St. Petersburg Times 5-22-79*

It's electrifying

You got me which packs a bigger voltage punch. Is it. . . ?

1. Florida's electric chair
2. A lightning bolt
3. Static cling

 A lightning bolt packs roughly 1 billion volts; Old Sparky, Florida's electric chair, about 2,000. *Knight-Ridder Report 7-9-93*

Visitors to the Fountain of Youth, St. Petersburg, 1951

PONCE UPON A TIME ...

Chapter 8

Europeans Behaving Badly—Explorers in Florida

The 1st Thanksgiving service in America was held on June 30, 1564, by—you got me! Was it. . . ?
1. **The English**
2. **The Spanish**
3. **The French**

French Huguenots, who established Fort Caroline on the St. Johns River near Jacksonville. *Tampa Tribune 4-30-72*

When you care enough to send the very best

Hernando de Soto led 600 men in his northward trek through Florida searching for riches (not counting the native "carriers"—actually, slaves—whom they got by seizing village chiefs along the way and forcing them to come across with food and men). Near Apalachee Bay he sent a present to his wife, Doña Isabel, in Cuba—but you got me what he sent her! Did he send. . . ?
1. **1,000 pearls from the bay**
2. **Indians**
3. **His left pinky toe**

De Soto sent 20 Native American women to his wife. *De Soto National Memorial brochure*

English admiral Sir Francis Drake, who looted and burned St. Augustine (and even went so far as to uproot the orange trees) in 1586, was best known for circumnavigating the globe in his flagship *The Golden Hind*—but you got me what *The Golden Hind* was called before Drake renamed it! Was she. . . ?

1. *The Flamingo*
2. *The Mockingbird*
3. *The Pelican*

The Golden Hind was formerly *The Pelican. Encyclopedia Britannica* and *Tampa Tribune 6-24-59*

Women and children first
Although Virginia Dare (b. August 18, 1587) is often considered the 1st child born in the New World, more correctly she was the 1st English child born here. The 1st European children born here were the 8 to 10 babies born on the St. Johns River 2 decades before Virginia Dare. But you got me what descent they were! Were they. . . ?
   1. Spanish
   2. French
   3. Portuguese

They were French. *Tampa Tribune 4-30-72*

Eurotrash in history
One intrepid explorer, who led the 1st large party of Europeans to enter the U.S., was described by Marjory Stoneman Douglas as "a red-headed one-eyed, hollow-voiced bully whom Cortes had thrown in jail. . . ." But you got me who that bully was! Was he. . . ?
   1. Hernando de Soto
   2. Panfilo de Narvaez
   3. Pedro Menendez

Panfilo de Narvaez. *Tampa Tribune 4-11-71*

Early fights for the right to party
In 1564 the French settlement of La Caroline was supposed to be an experimental settlement where the Huguenots would be granted the right to practice—you got me what! Was it. . . ?
   1. Protestantism
   2. Polygamy
   3. Vinification

La Caroline was an experiment in religious tolerance for the French Protestants. *[www.mindspring.com]*

It's an explorer thing

In 1565 Admiral Pedro Menéndez de Avilés was sent by King Philip II to remind the French settlers at La Caroline that Spain had laid claim to *all* of Florida. After a storm scuttled the French fleet, Menéndez rounded up the shipwreck survivors and, by way of reminding them, he—you got me! Did he. . . ?

1. **Deport them**
2. **Hack them to death**
3. **Sell them into slavery**

The Spanish butchered 300-plus French to death with swords. The place came to be called Matanzas, meaning slaughter. *Encyclopedia Britannica and [www.mindspring.com]*

The 1st European to kick the bucket in America is said to have done so in Charlotte Harbor—but you got me how he went! Was it. . . ?

1. **Malaria**
2. **Gator attack**
3. **Indian arrows**

 Indian arrows. *Boone's Florida Historical Markers and Sites by Floyd E. Boone*

 Seminole man and woman, circa 1950

Chapter 9

Gone Native American—Florida's Indians

When the Spanish explorers 1st set foot in Florida, the Native American population was estimated to be about—you got me! Was it. . . ?
1. **About 1,000**
2. **About 10,000**
3. **About 100,000**

Ten thousand was the estimated native population. By March 1843, only 360 Indians were left in Florida. *WPA Guide to Florida and Fort Brooke, A History by Donald L. Chamberlin*

Gimme shelter
The flag of Florida's Seminole tribe shows a traditional palm-thatched, open-sided hut—but you got me what that hut is called! Is it. . . ?
1. **Henee**
2. **Chickee**
3. **Turkee**

Chickee, also spelled chikkee. *Florida Handbook 1997–1998*

Hypoluxo, the name of an island in Lake Worth, is a Native American word—but you got me what it means! Is it. . . ?
1. **"Big water all around, no get out"**
2. **"No trespassing"**
3. **"High land"**

"Big water all around, no get out." *Yesterday's Palm Beach by Stuart B. McIver*

General Andrew Jackson pursued this Indian chief across Dixie County, finally capturing him and bringing the First Seminole War to a close.

But you got me who this great Seminole chief was! Was he. . . ?
   1. Chief Geronimo
   2. Chief Billie Bowlegs
   3. Chief Micanopy

Chief Billie Bowlegs. *Know Florida (State of Florida)*

Legend has it that the Calusa Indians (one of the Native American tribes in Florida in Columbus's day) made their last stand in what is now Pasco County. The Calusas made human sacrifices to their God, Toya—but you got me what Toya was God of! Was he. . . ?
   1. Sun God
   2. Panther God
   3. God of the Harvest

Sun God. The last 80 families of Calusas left for Cuba in 1762. *Know Florida (State of Florida) and Tampa Tribune 2-23-64*

In the money
According to 1998 reported statistics, each of the 2,440 members of the Seminole tribe receives $1,500 a month from—you got me! Is it. . . ?
   1. The Bureau of Indian Affairs
   2. The Park Service for the Everglades lease
   3. Bingo

Bingo and gaming revenues pay out a reported $1,500 to each tribe member. *Weekly Planet Apr 30–May 6, 1998*

During the Second Seminole War (1835–1842), captured Seminoles were shipped out to the Creek Reservation in Indian Territory (now Oklahoma)—but you got me what part of Florida was the last that many of them ever saw! Was it. . . ?
   1. Fort Pickens on Santa Rosa Island (Pensacola)
   2. Fort Brooke (Tampa)
   3. Fort Jefferson on Garden Key (Dry Tortugas)

Many Seminoles were put on ships at Fort Brooke. *St. Petersburg Times 6-21-87 and Encyclopedia Britannica*

Easy for you to say
You got me what small thing is called *in-ka-its-ho-chee-wa-chee* in the Seminole language! Is it. . . ?

1. Your pinky
2. A sleeper in your eye
3. A zit

Pinky. *The Seminoles of Florida by Minnie Moore-Willson*

If you don't look good, we don't look good
One of the aboriginal Indian tribes encountered by the early
Europeans were the Timucuans, who the Europeans reported stood 6
to 7 feet tall (skeletal remains say about 5'6" in reality). The men
wore their hair in top-knots and the women draped themselves in
Spanish moss. Certain Timucuans were heavily tattooed from neck to
ankles—but you got me who! Were they. . . ?
1. Leaders
2. Prisoners of War
3. Thieves

Leaders. *Forum: The Magazine of the Florida Humanities Council
Spring/Summer 1993 and St. Petersburg Times 5-15-83*

You only get one chance to make a good first impression
Instead of shaking hands, the traditional Seminole greeting when 2
men meet is to grasp each other by the—you got me! Is it. . . ?
1. Elbow
2. Throat
3. Ear

Elbow. *Tampa Tribune 5-9-59*

Someday my prints will come
The earliest known photo of a Seminole Indian is an 1852 ambrotype,
made in Washington or New York, on the occasion of negotiations
with authorities about the westward migration of the Seminoles. But
you got me who it's a picture of! Is it. . . ?
1. Osceola
2. Billy Bowlegs II
3. Alligator Boy

Billy Bowlegs II. *Tampa Tribune 2-28-60*

South Florida's 1st manufacturing industry involved the commercial production of something introduced to the white man by the Seminole Indians—but you got me what! Was it. . . ?
1. **Coontie flour**
2. **Sugar**
3. **Alligator-leather goods**

Coontie flour, or arrowroot cornstarch, was commercially produced in the Tampa and Miami areas. *Tampa Times 2-2-63 and Florida Wildlife Mar/Apr 1981*

Florida has 6 Native American reservations—but you got me how many tribes! Are there. . . ?
1. **1**
2. **2**
3. **6**

Two recognized by the Feds: the Miccosukee and the Seminoles. *Florida Handbook 1997–1998*

Would you like that original or extra-crispy?
Charismatic chief of the Seminole Indian tribe, James Billie, was hauled into Federal court in 1983 for killing and barbequing an endangered and protected Florida panther. Billie was exonerated but claimed that the panther tasted like—you got me! Was it. . . ?
1. **Chicken**
2. **A Big Mac**
3. **A cross between manatee and bald eagle**

Billie claimed the endangered panther tasted like a cross between manatee and bald eagle. *Weekly Planet Apr 30–May 6, 1998*

Pensacola was named for the local Indian tribe the Pansfalaya—but you got me what the name means! Is it. . . ?
1. **Hair People**
2. **Cabbage Eaters**
3. **Smiley Faces**

Hair People, or Long-Haired People. *Dictionary of the American Indian by John L. Stoutenburgh Jr.*

Bad hair days in history

Something belonging to Seminole Indian chief Osceola, famed as a brilliant military strategist in the Seminole Wars of the 1830s, ended up in a New York museum—but you got me what! Was it. . . ?

1. His head
2. His favorite cow
3. His battle dress

His head. Osceola died at age 33 in prison at Fort Moultrie, SC. An army surgeon removed his head, which later ended up in a museum of pathological exhibits at a NY med school. *Tampa Tribune-Times 11-3-68 and Tampa Tribune 10-17-71*

March madness

A Seminole war party headed by Jumper, Alligator, and Micanopy massacred the U.S. Army column led by Maj. Francis Langhorne Dade as they marched from Ft. Brooke on Tampa Bay toward Ft. King (now Ocala) on December 28, 1835. Less than 2 months later a more famous seige and massacre erupted elsewhere—but you got me what! Was it. . . ?

1. The Alamo
2. The *Maine*
3. Custer's Last Stand

The 12-day seige at the Alamo lasted from Feb 23–Mar 6, 1836, 40 years before Custer got his in 1876. The *Maine* exploded in 1898. *New Vistas Autumn 1975*

White man speak with forked tongue

The name of the great Seminole chief Osceola is a corruption of his true name, Asi-Yaholo, which means "shout siren when . . . "—you got me! When. . . ?

1. Being chased by wife
2. Stepping on sand spur
3. Drinking black drink

Asi-Yaholo translates "shout siren when drinking black drink." The black drink was probably the ritual beverage cassine, made from the *Ilex vomitoria* plant. *Tampa Tribune-Times 9-9-73 and Some Kind of Paradise by Mark Derr*

In 1917 Florida gave the Seminole Indians 99,000 acres for a reservation. There was one drawback to the place, but you got me what it
was! Was the place. . . ?
1. **In Jamaica**
2. **Largely underwater**
3. **An acre here, an acre there**

**The reservation had an average elevation of only 6 inches above sea
level and was flooded most of the time.** *Tampa Tribune-Times 9-9-73*

The Third Seminole War (also known as The Billy Bowlegs War,
1855–58) caused all but a few hundred of the Florida Indians to be
transported to one territory, where the 5 Great Southern Tribes had
been banished. But you got me where! Was it. . . ?
1. **The Montana Territory**
2. **The Oklahoma Territory**
3. **The Louisiana Purchase**

 The Oklahoma Territory. *Tampa Tribune-Times 9-9-73*

Chapter 10

Pardon Me, Do You Have Any Grey Poupon?—Florida's Founding Fathers

Fun couples in history

After the death of his 1st wife, Florida founding-father Henry Flagler married his nurse, Alice Shourds, whom he later divorced because she was a nut job, a fact which (if he didn't already know) he probably picked up on one morning at breakfast when she announced that she was engaged to be married to—you got me! Was it. . . ?

1. Isadora Duncan
2. The Czar of all the Russias
3. Her Welsh pony, Corky

The Czar. There was a state law prohibiting divorce from insane people, but Henry got the legislature to change that for him. *Florida's Past by Gene M. Burnett*

Miami got phone service in 1898. Among its 1st 25 subscribers were the likes of Henry Flagler and Julia Tuttle. But you got me how much a phone ran you per year! Was it. . . ?

1. $30 per month
2. $30 per year
3. $30 for lifetime service

$30 per year. *Florida Handbook 1997–1998*

All aboard

For Labor Day weekend 1935, $4 would get you a trip on Henry Flagler's Florida East Coast Railway from Miami to—you got me! Was it. . . ?

1. Daytona Beach
2. St. Augustine
3. Key West

Key West. The Labor Day Hurricane that slammed into the Keys in 1935 (the most powerful ever to hit the U.S.) wiped out the railroad. What was left of the roadbed was used to build the Overseas Highway. *Update Aug 1975 and St. Petersburg Times 8-11-98*

🎣 BONUS railroad question

According to a newspaper item from 1902, railroad magnate Henry M. Flagler decreed that one group of people could always ride his trains for free—but you got me who! Was it. . . ?

1. Expectant mothers
2. Seminole Indians
3. Soldiers

Flagler believed that the Seminole Indians had been so cheated and mistreated that he issued an order giving them free passage on the Flagler railroads. *Tampa Tribune 6-20-54*

John D. Rockefeller moved full-time to Ormond Beach in the 1930s, passed away there just short of his 98th birthday in 1937, and was buried in Cleveland. But you got me what's so notable about his Cleveland tomb! Is it that it's. . . ?

1. Solid gold
2. An unmarked pauper's grave
3. Bombproof

Rockefeller's tomb is bombproof. His Ormond Beach house was called The Casements. *New Yorker 5-11-98*

Carl Fisher, the man who helped establish Miami Beach, was also the developer behind a well-known racetrack—but you got me which one! Was it. . . ?

1. Churchill Downs
2. Daytona Speedway
3. Indianapolis Motor Speedway

Indianapolis Motor Speedway. *Highlights of Greater Miami 1946 by J. Calvin Mills*

The land before Bill Gates
According to *Fortune* magazine, in 1978 there were only 2 modern living American billionaires, one of whom was the largest individual landowner in Florida, who conducted his business from a hotel coffee shop. He was John D . . . you got me! Was it. . . ?
1. Rockefeller
2. MacArthur
3. Gates

John D. MacArthur made his business fortune in insurance as owner of Bankers Life and Casualty. Incidentally, his brother, Charles, co-wrote the play *The Front Page. Tampa Tribune 1-7-78 and New York Times 1-7-78*

It's always the quiet ones
A major architect of the 1920s, Addison Mizner is credited with introducing the shopping center to the state and also gave us another staple of Florida architecture—but you got me what! Was it. . . ?
1. The Florida room
2. Mobile homes
3. The carport

Mizner is credited with introducing the "Florida room." *Tampa Tribune 9-4-77*

🏊 BONUS Mizner question
Tucked away off Via Mizner, the shopping center named for famed architect Addison Mizner, on swanky Worth Avenue in Palm Beach, is the grave of Johnny Brown. But you got me who or what Johnny Brown was! Was it. . . ?
1. Mizner's faithful family retainer
2. Mizner's appendix
3. Mizner's pet monkey

The tomb reads: JOHNNY BROWN, THE HUMAN MONKEY in honor of Mizner's pet. *Tampa Tribune 9-4-77*

George Merrick, the developer behind Coral Gables, took a post in Miami in 1940 that he held until his death—but you got me what position! Was it. . . ?
1. Postmaster
2. Dogcatcher
3. Mayor

Merrick (1886–1942), who was one of the founders of The University of Miami, served as Miami's postmaster. *Who Was Who in Florida by Henry S. Marks*

Big deal
In 1881 Hamilton Disston became the nation's largest landowner when he gobbled up 4 million acres of Florida. But you got me what he paid per acre! Was it. . . ?

1. 25¢
2. $1
3. $5.50

25¢ per, or $1 million for 4 million acres. *Some Kind of Paradise by Mark Derr*

An American in Paris
When the Eiffel Tower was dedicated in Paris for the Centennial Exposition of 1889 (the centennial of the French Revolution), a Florida hotel magnate was asked to run up the 1st American flag flown on it. But you got me who that was! Was he. . . ?

1. Henry Flagler
2. Henry B. Plant
3. Henry Ford

 Henry B. Plant, who built the Tampa Bay Hotel, ran up the 1st American flag. *Florida's Promoters by Charles E. Horner*

Woman with dead shark, Atlantic Beach, Jacksonville, circa 1920

Chapter 11

Let's Do Something Cheap and Superficial—A Chop Suey of Florida Stuff

Sale of the century

Compass East was the name given to a top-secret project in which some 27 thousand–plus acres were picked up for a song at an average price of less than $200 per acre—but you got me what the land was being bought for! Was it. . . ?

1. The Kennedy Space Center
2. Everglades National Park
3. Disney World

Disney World. It was so hush-hush that all mail between Florida and the California Disney people was sent via a Kansas City post-office box. *Vinyl Leaves: Walt Disney World and America by Stephen M. Fjellman*

Caller, are you there?

It wasn't "a dime a minute" in 1933. A long-distance call would run you $7.75 (day rate) to call from Tampa and talk for 3 minutes to— you got me where! Was it. . . ?

1. Los Angeles
2. New York
3. Havana

Los Angeles cost $7.75 for 3 minutes between 4:30 A.M. and 7 P.M.; Havana cost $7.15; New York, $3.75. *Travel by Telephone: Some Selected Long Distance Rates from Tampa, Fla. July 1933*

You've got mail

In the early 1800s, before the days of the "barefoot mailmen," a letter mailed from Miami to Jupiter, 80 miles away, had to go 1st to Key West, then on to Cuba, then to New York, and then back. But you got me how long that letter took to get to Jupiter! Was it. . . ?

1. 6–8 days
2. 6–8 weeks
3. 6–8 months

6–8 weeks. *Florida Trend Oct 83*

You may already be a winner

In September 1988, Sheelah Ryan, 63, came into $55.16 million—but you got me how! Did she. . . ?

1. Hit the Florida Lottery
2. Won the nation's 1st ever tobacco suit
3. Happened upon the wreck of the galleon *Atocha*

Ryan won what was at the time the largest jackpot ever won in a state lottery. She will receive $2,213,968.80 (after taxes) every year for 20 years. *Facts on File 9-9-88*

In 135 B.C., Simon the Maccabee, in Judea, issued the 1st coin showing one of these—but you got me what! Is it a. . . ?

1. Flamingo
2. Citrus fruit
3. Chaise lounge

The coinage showed a citron, probably the 1st citrus fruit to reach western Asia. *Tampa Tribune 11-29-39*

More bang for your buck

According to the game laws in effect in 1934, a hunter could bag 1 deer, 15 quail, 2 turkeys, and 18 doves in one day without going afoul of the law—but you got me how many Florida panthers he could kill! Was it. . . ?

1. None
2. 1
3. As many as he wanted

Panthers were unprotected, as were alligators, bears, and wildcats; so as many as he wanted. *The Florida Conservator Nov 1934*

🎣 BONUS hunting question
In 1859 hunting in Florida was prohibited on—you got me! Was it. . . ?
1. Horseback
2. Months ending with an *r*
3. Sunday

Sunday. *Cycle of a Century in Game Legislation in Florida*

Feeding time
You got me whether or not breastfeeding in public is legal in Florida!
1. It's legal
2. It's a misdemeanor
3. Nursing mothers face felony charges for lewd and lacivious behavior

In 1993 Governor Lawton Chiles (1930–1998) made it legal to breast-feed in public. *Facts on File 4-8-93*

Who put the goober in gubernatorial?
On a tour of Tokyo in 1965, Florida governor Haydon Burns went around handing out "Instant Florida" promotional kits that contained something live—but you got me what! Was it. . . ?
1. Live orange-tree sprigs
2. Live flamingo chicks
3. Live baby "gators"

Live baby Florida gators, although they were most likely South American caimans—not real gators. *Tampa Tribune 9-21-66*

In Pensacola, people get in line as early as 2:30 in the morning and wait up to 15 hours to get into—you got me! Is it the. . . ?
1. Naval Aviation Museum
2. Gulf Islands National Seashore
3. Brownsville Revival

The Brownsville Revival is one of the longest-running revivals in the history of the Pentacostal movement. *Detroit Free Press 10-11-97 and Pensacola News Journal 11-20-97*

The Florida State Legislature has proclaimed the 1st of August to be—you got me! Is it. . . ?
1. Possum Day
2. Say "Thanks, Mom" Day
3. Eat-a-Jelly-Donut Day

Possum Day. The town of Chipley calls itself the Possum Capital of the U.S. [www.roadsideamerica.com]

The term "cracker" refers to natives of the Florida mainland. But you got me what term is applied to people born in the Keys! Is it. . . ?
1. Conchs
2. Razorbacks
3. Grovers

Conchs. "Cracker" is derived from the bullwhip cracks associated with the early industries of turpentining and logging; today, it's the rough equivalent of "redneck." WPA Guide to Florida

Dress down
West central Florida (Pasco County in particular) lays claim to the title of Nudist Capital of America—but you got me what percentage of the members of those colonies are over 35 years old! Is it. . . ?
1. About 30%
2. About 60%
3. About 90%

92% of members are over 35. Median incomes are around $50,000, and 77% have gone to college. Weekly Planet 5-29 to 6-3-98

A Mrs. Vivian Laramore Rader, hailing from Miami, served in this official capacity from her appointment in 1931 until the end of her life in 1973—but you got me what she was! Was she. . . ?
1. Cook at the Governor's Mansion
2. Miss Florida Orange Blossom
3. Poet Laureate of Florida

She followed Franklin N. Wood as the Poet Laureate. Dr. Edmund Skellings took the reins in 1980. Florida Handbook 1997–1998

Home sweet home
A common vernacular house style in urban areas originated in Africa

and got its name because a shot fired from the front door could supposedly go out the back without hitting anything. But you got me what those houses are called! Are they. . . ?
1. Shotgun houses
2. Cannon houses
3. Musket houses

Shotgun houses. *Florida Heritage Magazine, Spring 1996 [www.dos.state.fl.us]*

The last time most people saw this boat, she was sinking after getting shot up by the German gunboat, the *Louisa*. But now she's on display in Key Largo. The boat is—you got me!
1. The *Bounty*
2. The *African Queen*
3. The *Pequod*

The *African Queen*. *St. Petersburg Times 10-25-81 and Tampa Tribune 2-15-82*

We must, we must, we must improve the bust
According to the American Society of Plastic and Reconstructive Surgeons, the states of Florida, Texas, and California have the most breast enhancements; but the women in one of those states want bigger implants—but you got me which state! Is it. . . ?
1. Florida
2. Texas
3. California

It's Texas, of course, where everything's bigger. *New York Times 7-21-98*

Bum steer
According to one old cracker superstition, sticking a fork in milk would make a cow do something at milking time—but you got me what! Was it. . . ?
1. Kick
2. Croak
3. Not give any milk

Kick. *Tampa Tribune 5-15-55*

🦀 BONUS superstition question

In Florida's territorial days, superstitious girls cooked what were called "dumb suppers" (meals prepared in silence) in order to see if something was in their future—but you got me what! Was it. . . ?
1. Riches
2. Travel
3. A husband

A husband. *Tampa Tribune 9-16-57*

Some are named "Ferrari," "Minilee," and "Tiffany"—but you got me what they are! Are they. . . ?
1. Florida lieutenant governors
2. Watermelons
3. The oldest streets in St. Augustine

They're Florida watermelon varieties. *[http://hammock.ifas.ufl.edu]*

🦀 BONUS watermelon question

Florida is the nation's leading producer of watermelons. According to early 1990s stats, you got me how many pounds of watermelon the average person eats! Is it. . . ?
1. 4 pounds
2. 14 pounds
3. 24 pounds

14 pounds, up from 12 in the early '80s. *[www.act.fcic.usda.gov]*

Movers and shakers

You got me what caused the churchbells in St. Augustine to start ringing on August 31, 1886! Was it. . . ?
1. The swallows on their way to Capistrano
2. An earthquake
3. A heat wave caused the brass to crack

The Charleston earthquake. *Tampa Tribune 7-9-83*

Florida's Great Seal shows a steamboat and a palm tree (cocoa, some say)—but you got me who the person on the seal is! Is it. . . ?
1. Andrew Jackson, the 1st territorial governor
2. Ponce de León
3. A Native American woman

The Great Seal shows a Native American woman holding a flower garland that hangs to the ground (some say she's scattering flowers). *Florida Highways June 1945*

Don't leave home without it
In Ybor City in 1905, the sidewalks were wooden planks; so was the floor of The Columbia, said to be the oldest Spanish restaurant in the country. But you got me whether men walked around wearing sidearms in those days!
1. They sure did
2. No way; carrying sidearms got you a night in the pokey
3. Men carried knives, but never guns

In 1905 men openly wore guns in holsters; the ladies wore long dresses with bustles. Single men paid $5 a month to eat at The Columbia. *Tampa Tribune 10-5-80 and 9-25-94*

Beat the Bush
After losing a close race for the governorship to Lawton Chiles in 1994, Jeb Bush did something that he says changed his life—but you got me what! Was it. . . ?
1. Married wife #4
2. Changed his religion
3. Pierced his belly button

Jeb Bush converted to Roman Catholicism. *St. Petersburg Times 6-7-98*

BONUS none-of-your-business religion question
From the time Florida was granted statehood in 1845 up to 1999, there have been 39 governors, and the greatest number of those were—you got me! Was it. . . ?
1. Episcopalian
2. Baptist
3. Congregationalist

15 have been Episcopalian, 9 Baptist, and 3 Congregationalist (other denominations represented include: Presbyterian (6 governors), Methodist (5), and Roman Catholic (2, including Governor Bush). *St. Petersburg Times 6-7-98*

Before the railroad was extended to Tampa and Cedar Key went downhill, the Eagle and Faber companies had factories there to pre-pare cedar wood for making—you got me! Was it. . . ?
1. Dentures
2. Pencils
3. The world's finest wine barrels

Eagle and Faber made lead pencils out of the extensive cedar forests. *WPA Guide to Florida*

For whom the Taco Bell tolls: Florida food

Betcha can't eat just one
You got me whether flamingo tongues were ever served at the sumptuous banquets of Roman emperors!
1. Flamingo tongues were a favorite dish
2. Romans had never even seen a flamingo
3. Flamingoes don't have tongues

Flamingo tongues were a favorite dish, along with ostrich wings and songbird, but they never saw an orange. *Caesar and Christ by Will Durant and Tampa Tribune 9-25-55*

Hold the mayo
You got me how many delis there are in Florida where you can get a hot pastrami on rye! Is it. . . ?
1. About 100
2. About 1,000
3. About 10,000

With approximately 1,090, according to the GTE Superpages Interactive Services (1998), Florida ranks 4th among the states behind New York's approx. 4,440, California's approx. 3,320, and New Jersey's approx. 2,759. *The Jewish Book of Lists by Joel Samberg*

Turkey is the traditional centerpiece of American Thanksgiving dinners—but you got me what's the centerpiece at a traditional *Nochebuena* dinner on Christmas Eve in Cuban households! Is it. . . ?
1. Goose
2. Roast suckling pig
3. Rack of lamb

Roast suckling pig, called *lechon asado. Miami Spice by Stephen Raichlen*

Would you like fries with that?

You got me what's the only brand of fast food you can get at Disney parks! Is it. . . ?

1. Pizza Hut
2. McDonald's
3. Kentucky Fried Chicken

McDonald's. *St. Petersburg Times 1-10-98*

My bologna has a first name, it's R-O-V-E-R

Travelling through Florida in 1540, Hernando de Soto's army had the hogs that they brought with them from Cuba, but their favorite meat dish was—you got me! Was it. . . ?

1. Wild turkey
2. Bass
3. Dog

Their favorite meat dish was "little dog." *Tampa Tribune 10-6-57*

You are what you eat

Literally translated, the name of the meat dish called *vaca frita* means—you got me! Is it. . . ?

1. Lamb's tail
2. Fried cow
3. Mouse whiskers

It means "fried cow." *Cassell's Spanish Dictionary*

Tossed cookies

The Gulf island, Anna Maria Island near St. Petersburg, was developed by Charles Martin Roser, the Ohio cracker and candy manufacturer who created a popular cookie. But you got me what cookie! Is it. . . ?

1. Oreo
2. Fig Newton
3. Chips Ahoy

National Biscuit Company (Nabisco) bought Roser out in 1910 for a reported cool million to get his Fig Newtons. *Tampa Tribune-Times 8-1-76*

Florida in grapefruit and oranges, Cypress Gardens
postcard, circa 1950

Chapter 12

The Dusty Details—A Quick Check of Recent Florida History

Come to where the flavor is
Around 1841 the United States, under the Armed Occupation Act, offered to anyone who would live in Florida—you got me! Was it. . . ?
1. 12 bottles of Kentucky whiskey
2. 160 acres
3. 2 mules

160 acres. James Stevens sold his 160 acres, the greater part of Clearwater, for the price of one slave. *Clearwater Sun 5-29-80*

When the Second Seminole War was declared over and done with by the U.S. in 1842, the recognized chief of the Florida Seminole people was Holata Micco, who was better known as—you got me! Was he. . . ?
1. Billy Bowlegs
2. Billy Bowarms
3. Billy Bopeep

Chief Billy Bowlegs belonged to the "Cowkeeper Dynasty" and was one of the Seminole royals. He also led the Third Seminole War (1855–1858) and fought for the Union during the Civil War. *Who Was Who in Florida by Henry S. Marks*

Party like it's 1845
In 1845, when Florida was granted statehood, the 2 political parties were the Democrats (or Locofoco) and the—you got me! Was it. . . ?
1. Whigs
2. Republicans
3. Federalists

Whigs. In the 1st state election, 5,989 votes were cast. *Florida State Chamber of Commerce 1945*

On March 3, 1845, both Florida (as a slave state) and Iowa (as a free state) were granted statehood by the 10th U.S. president on his last day in office. But you got me who he was! Was he. . . ?
1. John Tyler
2. Benjamin Harrison
3. James Monroe

John Tyler, who brought the Second Seminole War (1835–1842) to a close and established the U.S. Weather Bureau. *Chronicle of America and Encyclopedia Britannica*

They're playing our song
In 1845 the new state of Florida was ushered into the Union by raising the U.S. and state flags, firing cannon, and playing the song called—you got me! Was the song. . . ?
1. "The Star-Spangled Banner"
2. "Yankee Doodle"
3. "Jeannie with the Light Brown Hair"

"Yankee Doodle." *Florida State Chamber of Commerce 1945*

At the time when statehood was granted in 1845, you got me who had governed Florida the longest! Was it. . . ?
1. The Spanish
2. The British
3. The Americans

Florida had been under Spanish rule for 236 years, British for 20, American 24. *Sun Dial Dec 1945*

Pride of the Yankees
After lightly firing on Tampa in April 1862, you got me what the Union commander did! Did he. . . ?
1. March his forces into the city
2. Surrender
3. Send a note of apology

He sent an apology. 2 years later, Union forces walked in without firing a shot while the local homeguard was off on a cattle drive. *St. Petersburg Times 6-21-87*

On May 17, 1869, a commission appointed by the Florida legislature agreed to do something with "that portion of Florida lying west of the Chattahoochee and Apalachicola rivers . . . "—but you got me what! Was it. . . ?
1. Sell it to Alabama for a cool mil
2. Designate it as the nation's 1st wildlife refuge area
3. Form an independent homeland for freed slaves

They agreed to sell it to Alabama, but carpetbaggers in the legislature put the kibosh on the deal. *Tampa Tribune 9-15-59*

Sounds like a plan
A letter in the National Archives revealed that the Confederate War Department had a unique battle plan in its files to defeat Federal ships at Pensacola—but you got me what the plan was! Was it. . . ?
1. Drop poison-gas bombs from balloons
2. Flood the town with women and cheap booze
3. Infest the wooden hulls with termites

Dropping poison-gas bombs from balloons. *Civil War Times [www.thehistorynet.com]*

The Dry Tortugas (*tortugas* is Spanish for turtles) Light Station was one of only a handful of lighthouses that was kept lighted during the Civil War. But you got me who held it! Was it. . . ?
1. The North
2. The South
3. Cuba

Federal troops (the North) occupied the Keys during the Civil War. *Tampa Times-Tribune 11-20-77*

On September 27, 1864, a local militia of young boys under 16 and men as old as 75 fought the Battle of Marianna against overwhelming Union forces. But you got me what that home guard was called! Was it. . . ?

1. The Cradle to Grave Company
2. The Pops and Pups Guard
3. The Old Hat Regiment

The Cradle to Grave Company. *Tampa Tribune 9-26-71*

Clear as mud

A Maryland country doctor set the broken leg of John Wilkes Booth, not knowing that the man had shot Lincoln. Convicted of complicity, the doctor was sentenced to serve life at Fort Jefferson in the Dry Tortugas. You got me what familiar cliché comes down to us from the good doctor! Is it. . . ?
1. Good Sam
2. His name is mud
3. Shake a leg

From Doctor Samuel Mudd came "his name is Mudd." For his service during a yellow fever epidemic, Mudd, after 4 years in prison, was pardoned by President Andrew Johnson in 1869. By some accounts, the phrase was in circulation before that time: From earlier British dialect, "mud" means "fool." *Tampa Times 5-3-74 and New Dictionary of American Slang*

On December 6, 1861, the name of New River County was changed to Bradford in honor of Capt. Richard G. Bradford, the 1st Florida officer killed in some war—but you got me which one! Was it. . . ?
1. The Spanish-American War
2. The Civil War
3. The War of 1812

Confederate officer Bradford was killed in the Battle of Santa Rosa Island, in 1861, during the Civil War. *Tampa Tribune 12-12-71*

Long shot

Although history books tell us that the 1st shots of the Civil War were fired at Fort Sumter, NC, on April 12, 1861, some say that the 1st shots were fired on January 8th—but you got me where! Was it. . . ?
1. Fort Barrancas
2. Fort Lauderdale
3. Fort Myers

Fort Barrancas (at what is today the Pensacola Naval Air Station).
Others say that the shots exchanged at Fort Pickens 5 days later were
the 1st. *AP 8-3-84*

All stations go

On February 20, 1864, the biggest Civil War battle fought in Florida
takes its name from the railroad station on the Florida, Atlantic, and
Gulf Railroad near where the battle was fought. But you got me what
station it was! Was it. . . ?

1. Olustee
2. Two Egg
3. Penn

The Battle of Olustee was fought near the Olustee station. It's also
called The Battle of Ocean Pond after the marsh north of the station.
The Yankees lost over 1,800 killed, wounded, or missing and termed
the battle "the second Dade Massacre." *Tampa Tribune 9-5-63 and 2-
27-72*

At the time of the Civil War, the state had roughly 78,000 white citi-
zens—but you got me how many people lived as slaves in Florida!
Was it. . . ?

1. 6,000
2. 16,000
3. 61,000

61,000 people. *Florida Trend May 1983*

During the Civil War, Tallahassee was 1 of only 2 Confederate state
capitals not captured by Union forces. But you got me what the other
was! Was it. . . ?

1. Augusta, Georgia
2. Dover, Delaware
3. Austin, Texas

Austin. *World Book Multimedia Encyclopedia*

On April 1, 1865, Democratic governor John Milton took his own life
with a shotgun after telling the legislature in his final message that
"death would be preferable to . . . "—you got me! Was it preferable
to. . . ?

1. State income tax
2. Reunion with the North
3. Living in Tallahassee

Milton didn't want to make nice after the Civil War. *St. Petersburg Times 12-13-98*

Old soldiers do so die
In September 1957 when William A. Lundy, Florida's last Confederate Army vet, passed away at age 109—you got me how many Confederate vets were still alive! Was it. . . ?
1. Lundy was the last
2. There were 2 others left
3. There were 6 others

There were 2: one man in Texas and another in Virginia; the last Union soldier had died in Minnesota in 1956. More than 16 thousand soldiers enlisted in Florida (1,200 for the North), and at least 5 thousand died of wounds or disease. *Tampa Tribune 9-2-57 and Florida: The Long Frontier by Marjory Stoneman Douglas*

What becomes a legend most
In February 1887 tourists were allowed to visit the Wild West legend who spent 18 months jailed at Fort Pickens in Pensacola—but you got me who! Was it. . . ?
1. Geronimo
2. Belle Star
3. Butch Cassidy

Geronimo, and a small band of Chiricahua Apaches. *At the Water's Edge by William Warren Rogers and Lee Willis*

Bonus Geronimo question
Geronimo's Indian name was *Goyathlay*, which means—you got me! Was it. . . ?
1. "Little teapot"
2. "One who yawns"
3. "One with ants in his pants"

"One who yawns." *Encyclopedia Britannica*

A wop bop a loo bop a lop bam BOOM!

At 7 P.M., August 14, 1888, three cannons fired off 50 rounds in the streets of Jacksonville. But you got me why! Was it. . . ?

1. To put down a union-organizing effort at The National Container Corp.
2. To destroy yellow fever "germs"
3. The South was rising again

During the yellow fever epidemic of 1888, cannons were fired in the belief that the concussion would kill the "fomites" (germs) that carried the disease. Walter Reed, for whom the Washington, D. C., hospital is named, is credited with proving that yellow fever was transmitted by *Aëdes aegypti* mosquitoes. *All Florida TV Week Magazine 10-14-61 and Encyclopedia Britannica*

Good night, nurse

Clara Barton spent time in Tampa during the Spanish-American War in 1898 as head of the American Red Cross. She resigned from that association on May 14, 1904, because she'd been criticized for—you got me! Was it. . . ?

1. Her views on planned parenthood
2. Poor bookkeeping
3. Assisting suicides

Poor bookkeeping, as well as "inattention to administrative details." *St. Petersburg Times 7-6-81*

On March 28, 1898, the ship *Olivette* landed in Tampa, bringing the survivors from some famous ship. But you got me which one! Was it. . . ?

1. The *Titantic*
2. The *Lusitania*
3. The *Maine*

"Remember the *Maine*," the U.S. battleship that blew up in Havana harbor? In 1898 a Spanish mine was believed to have caused the explosion that killed 265 crewmen; in 1976 experts concluded that the explosion was caused by a fire in a coal bunker that ignited munitions. *Florida's Promoters by Charles E. Horner and St. Petersburg Times 2-15-98*

Unhappy campers
In 1898 the expeditionary force of 30,000 that bivouacked around Tampa for the Spanish-American War was the largest ever put together for combat abroad. But you got me what killed the greatest numbers of soldiers in that war! Was it. . . ?
1. **The Battle of San Juan Hill**
2. **Hurricane Edward**
3. **Sickness**

Battle deaths in that war numbered around 385; sicknesses, like yellow fever (called "yellow jack"), killed over 2,000. *Florida's Promoters by Charles E. Horner and St. Petersburg Times 2-15-98*

🦀 BONUS 1898 question
La Culebra (meaning "The Snake") was the favorite of troops bivouacked in Tampa before embarking to Cuba for the Spanish-American War—but you got me the favorite what! Was *La Culebra* their favorite. . . ?
1. **Saloon**
2. **Ship**
3. **Woman of ill-repute**

La Culebra **was the soldiers' favorite working girl.** *St. Petersburg Times 6-21-87*

In Cuba, February 24th is celebrated as the day its fight for liberation from Spain began in 1895. The secret message in which the Cuban Revolutionary Junta (in NY) ordered that battle was smuggled to Havana from West Tampa inside a—you got me! Was it a. . . ?
1. **Cigar**
2. **Ladies bustle**
3. **Long beard**

Blas O'Halloran, a cigar factory owner, rolled the message stating that the battle should begin no sooner than mid-February into a cigar, plugged it in his mouth, and waltzed through Cuban customs. *St. Petersburg Times 6-21-87*

On November 11, 1918, the Miami Fire Department blew its siren continuously and fired off its cannon, starting at 3 in the morning. But you got me why! Was it. . . ?
1. **The Great Miami Fire**

2. The end of World War I
3. The arrival of Henry Flagler's East Coast Railroad

It was Armistice Day, ending WWI. *Update Oct 1975*

The 19th Amendment to the U.S. Constitution (granting women the right to vote) was ratified by 38 states and became part of the Constitution in August 1920. But you got me when the Florida legislature got around to ratifying it! Was it. . . ?
1. 1921
2. 1932
3. 1969

On May 13, 1969, in a symbolic action, the Florida Legislature finally ratified the 19th Amendment. Of course, Florida women could vote right after the Secretary of State proclaimed ratification in 1920. *Florida Handbook 1997–1998*

The coast is clear
On Thursday, June 18, 1942, four men put ashore on Ponte Vedra Beach, southeast of Jacksonville. They walked out to the highway and caught a bus for Jacksonville—but you got me what was so unusual about that! Was it. . . ?
1. They'd been missing in the Bermuda Triangle for 25 years
2. They were German saboteurs
3. They were the world's only Siamese quadruplets

They were German saboteurs, 1 of 2 teams apprehended by the FBI. *"Undercover" by Harvey Ardman; World War II [www.the historynet.com]*

World War II German POWs (largely from Rommel's Africa Korps) spent the war working in a packing plant and a lumber camp at the 1st POW camp established in this neck of the woods. But you got me where it was! Was it. . . ?
1. Dry Tortugas
2. Dade City
3. At the present site of the Magic Kingdom

Dade City. More than 7,800 POWs, mostly Germans, were put to work in army camps, fields, and forests. *Tampa Morning Tribune 9-25-45*

⚓ BONUS WWII question

In 1942 German U-boats torpedoed 25 ships between Cape Canaveral and Key West, and even shot down one—you got me! Did a German sub shoot down a. . . ?

1. Blimp
2. Pan Am DC-3 en route to Havana
3. A replica of the Wright Brothers' Kitty Hawk Flyer

One of the blimps that aided the Navy patrols in their search for German subs. *Miami In Our Own Words by Nancy Acrum and Rich Bard, Eds.*

The very model of a modern major general

In November 1988 a four-star general was appointed head of the U.S. Central Command at MacDill AFB in Tampa—but you got me who that was! Was it. . . ?

1. Norman Schwarzkopf
2. Colin Powell
3. Henry Shelton

After Iraq invaded Kuwait on August 2, 1990, Schwarzkopf moved Central Command from Tampa to Riyadh before Operation Desert Storm. *Current Biography Yearbook 1991*

Making waves: flags over Florida

When Old Glory was 1st unfurled over St. Augustine on July 16, 1821 (and over Pensacola on July 21), when Spain handed Florida over to the U.S., you got me how many "stars" were on the Stars and Stripes! Was it. . . ?

1. 23
2. 33
3. 43

23. *The Florida Historical Society Quarterly Jan 1926*

Run it up the flagpole and see who salutes

Eight flags have flown over the 20-mile area from Fernandina to Mayport, including, in 1817, one that was a white banner with a green cross. But you got me whose flag that was! Was it. . . ?

1. The Republic of Mexico
2. The Republic of Florida
3. Scotsman, Sir Gregor MacGregor

Gen. Sir Gregor MacGregor, who served with Bolivar in South America, sailed into Fernandina with the big idea to liberate it from Spain and ran up his own flag. *St. Petersburg Times 2-29-76*

On September 21, 1817, French pirate Luis Aury annexed Amelia Island and raised the flag of—you got me! Was it. . . ?
1. Mexico
2. France
3. Texas

He flew the Mexican flag and threw Fernandina open to the illegal slave trade. *St. Petersburg Times 2-29-76 and Who Was Who in Florida by Henry S. Marks*

For nearly a year, the Canadian flag flew over the Florida state capitol, but you got me how come! Was it. . . ?
1. The Maple Leaf was the official state flag of Territorial Florida
2. Florida's 9th governor was Canadian-born
3. During the Iranian hostage crisis

In honor of the Canadian ambassador who rescued 6 Americans when Iranians seized the U.S. Embassy in Tehran. The flag flew until the crisis ended. *Florida Handbook 1997–1998*

Not that long may she wave
The Free and Independent State of West Florida lasted less than 3 months in 1810. Her flag was known as— you got me! Was it. . . ?
1. The Scarlett Flag
2. The Butler Flag
3. The Bonnie Blue Flag

The Bonnie Blue flag had a lone star on a blue field. The state was west of Florida's present borders. *Florida Handbook 1997–1998*

Florida's 1st state flag had 5 horizontal stripes of white, blue, orange, red, and green, and the words—you got me! Did it say. . . ?
1. **In God We Trust**
2. **Let Us Alone**
3. **The Sunshine State**

 Let Us Alone. The U.S. flag served as the union (the upper inner corner). *Florida State Chamber of Commerce 1945*

Chapter 13

We'll Leave the Light On for You—Florida Hotels and Other Places to Stay

Hunka hunka burnin' building

On March 18, 1925, Henry Flagler's 2nd Breakers hotel burned to the ground (the 1st one went up in smoke in 1903). But you got me what started the fire! Was it. . . ?

1. **A pelican bumped over a tiki torch**
2. **A hair curling iron**
3. **Flagler smoked cigars in bed**

A hair curling iron. *History of The Breakers [www.thebreakers.com]*

Bonus Breakers question

The Breakers boasts the oldest 18-hole golf course in Florida—but you got me what it's called! Is it. . . ?

1. **The Ocean Course**
2. **The Blue Monster**
3. **The Stadium Course**

The Ocean Course is Florida's oldest 18-hole course. *[www. thebreakers.com]*

The price is right

When St. Petersburg's grand hotel, The Vinoy, 1st opened on New Year's Eve 1925, its rooms were some of the priciest in the state. But you got me how much a room at The Vinoy would set you back! Was it. . . ?

Demolition of the Atlantis Hotel, Miami Beach, 1973

1. $20
2. $100
3. $220

Rooms went for $20 per night, meals included. Today it's the Renaissance Vinoy Resort. *Florida Heritage Magazine, Summer 1996 [www.dos.state.fl.us]*

Sticks and stones

Built originally out of flotsam and jetsam that washed ashore on Vero Beach, Waldo Sexton's beach house grew into an eclectic landmark hotel, but you got me which one! Is it. . . ?
1. The Driftwood Resort
2. The Castoff Inn
3. The Shipwreck B&B

The Driftwood Resort. Two of the old "driftwood" buildings are still there. *Tampa Tribune-Times 5-24-81*

During construction of the famed Tampa Bay Hotel, something had to be done to the bricks before they could be used—but you got me what! Did they have to be. . . ?
1. Fumigated
2. Dyed red
3. Broken in half

Part of the bricks that went into the Tampa Bay Hotel were made in Cincinnati and shipped via Jacksonville. Upon arrival in Tampa, they were fumigated because of Jacksonville's yellow fever outbreak. *Encyclopedia Britannica and The University of Tampa Foundation 1966*

Pre–itsy bitsy teenie weenie yellow polka dot bikinis

Before 1926, ladies going into the ocean at The Breakers beach were subject to the fish eye of the Beach Censor, who enforced the dress code. No skin could peek out between suit and stocking top, and all bathing costumes had to be—you got me! Was it. . . ?
1. Black
2. Silk
3. Waterproof

Black. Sometimes velvet with bows. *Palm Beach Scandals by Jack Owen*

Before making it big in Hollywood, one celebrity worked as a swimming instructor at Coral Gable's famed Biltmore Hotel—but you got me who! Was it. . . ?
1. Esther Williams
2. Fabio
3. Johnny Weismuller

Johnny Weismuller of *Tarzan* fame. *Florida—Eyewitness Travel Guides*

Key Largo boasts a 1st in the hotel world: The room is under 30 feet of—you got me! Is it. . . ?
1. Water
2. Dirt
3. Landfill

Jules' Undersea Lodge is anchored 30 feet underwater. *Fodor's 96: Miami & The Keys*

This entertainer fled the 1933 Cuban Revolution, attended St. Patrick's High School in Miami, and was discovered at the Roney-Plaza Hotel by "rumba king" Xavier Cugat—but you got me who he was! Was he. . . ?
1. Tito Puente
2. Desi Arnaz
3. Señor Wences

Desiderio Alberto Arnaz y de Acha 3d, aka Desi Arnaz. *Current Biography 1952*

Luck be a lady
Although gambling was illegal in Florida, that didn't stop Henry Flagler from opening a gambling parlor at one of his Palm Beach hotels. Only men were allowed in until 1899, when women were admitted as long as they were—you got me! As long as they were. . . ?
1. Married
2. Escorted by a gentleman
3. Nuns

Over Flagler's protest, escorted women were allowed in. *Some Kind of Paradise by Mark Derr*

In 1909 the Royal Palm Hotel had Miami's 1st and only one—but you got me 1st and only what! Was it. . . ?
1. **Swimming pool**
2. **Air conditioner**
3. **Flush toilet**

Swimming pool. *Miami 1909 by Thelma Peters*

Lifestyles of the rich and civil defense–minded
In addition to having 58 bedrooms and 33 bathrooms, Palm Beach's grandest mansion, Mar-a-lago, has 3 special living quarters—but you got me what they are! Are they. . . ?
1. **3 air-conditioned dog houses**
2. **3 bomb shelters**
3. 3 oak paneled private railway cars

Three bomb shelters. *Florida—Eyewitness Travel Guides*

Ceremony marking the restoration of the Normandy Isle fountain,
Miami Beach, 1970

Chapter 14

It's Not What You Know, It's Who— Florida People

We hear he is a whiz of a wiz: Edison in Florida

No pain, no gain

Although he believed that exercising his mind was the only workout that a body needed, Thomas Edison is credited with building in 1910 one of Florida's 1st modern—you got me! Was it. . . ?

1. A weight room
2. A jogging track
3. A swimming pool

Edison put in a swimming pool. *[www.dos.state.fl.us]*

Weird science

The "Green Laboratory" in Fort Myers was home to Thomas Edison's last big experiment in which "The Father of Modern Electronics" was trying to make—you got me what! Was it. . . ?

1. Beer
2. Rubber
3. Hair-growing tonic

He was trying to make rubber out of goldenrod. *Edison in Florida— The Green Laboratory by Olav Thulesius*

The lights are on, but nobody's home

Longtime winter resident of Fort Myers, Thomas Edison received his only formal schooling in Port Huron, Michigan, where, after only 3 months, the schoolmaster pronounced the future inventor of the incandescent electric light, the movie projector, and the phonograph as—you got me! Did he say Edison was. . . ?

1. "The greatest genius I've ever met"
2. "The wizard of Menlo Park"
3. "Retarded"

The schoolmaster expelled Edison as "retarded." *Encyclopedia Britannica*

Better living through chemistry

In 1980 Thomas Edison's laboratory (one of the high points of any tour of his winter home in Fort Myers) was put off limits by a government agency. But you got me how come! Was it because. . . ?
1. **Human bones were discovered under the floorboards**
2. **Of fear the chemicals would explode**
3. **President-elect Reagan assembled his cabinet there**

Because Edison had a photographic memory, he never labelled chemicals. The EPA and estate managers were concerned that the unknown substances might have become unstable. *St. Petersburg Times 4-26-81*

Edison had 2 homes built on his winter estate in Fort Myers because there's something that he did not like to do in the same house that he lived in—but you got me what! Was it. . . ?
1. **Bathe**
2. **See Mrs. Edison**
3. **Eat**

Edison so disliked the smell of cooking food that he lived in one house and ate in the other. *Thomas A. Edison Winter Home & Museum brochure*

Showbiz alfresco

Beware of Geeks

Twenty miles southeast of Tampa in Gibsonton, carny Grady Stiles Jr., a victim of the genetic condition known as ectrodactyly, was shot to death by his long-suffering wife and his son, "The Human Blockhead" (who drove nails up his nostrils for a living). On the carnival circuit, Stiles gained fame and fortune as—you got me! Was he. . . ?

1. The World's Only Living Half Man
2. Big Foot
3. Lobster Boy

Lobster Boy. *Lobster Boy by Fred Rosen*

That first step's a lulu

In San Juan, Puerto Rico, in 1978, when Karl Wallenda, the granddaddy of highwire performers, fell 10 stories to his death, flags throughout "Circus City" were flown at half-staff—but you got me what "Circus City" is! Is it. . . ?
1. Sarasota
2. Fort Myers
3. Homestead

Sarasota. Wallenda is buried in Manasota Memorial Park. *St. Petersburg Times 3-24-78*

Thirty years after his glamorous and extravagant Sarasota life ended in 1936, this multimillionaire's body was discovered moldering in a temporary crypt in Hackensack, NJ, and was headed for a pauper's grave. But you got me who he was! Was he. . . ?
1. P. T. Barnum
2. James Bailey
3. John Ringling

John Ringling and his wife, Mable, lay in crypts 28 and 33, forgotten. The bodies were relocated to Fairmont, NJ, and in June 1991 were interred on the grounds of their Sarasota home, Cà d'Zan. *Tampa Tribune 1-28-73*

In 1979 the circus world lost Emmett Kelly, who passed away at his Sarasota home after 50 years in poorly fitting trousers—but you got me what Kelly's clown character was named! Was he. . . ?
1. Sad Sack
2. Weary Willie
3. Floppy Freddy

Weary Willie. *St. Petersburg Times 4-1-79*

God rest you merry gentlemen
On North Boulevard in Tampa, a cemetery called Showmen's Rest serves as final resting place for members of a certain profession—but you got me what! Is it. . . ?
1. Carnies
2. Actors
3. Movie-theater projectionists

Outdoor showmen, aka carnies. *Tampa Times 2-17-78*

Give him the brush

Picture perfect
One of the classics of American painting, *The Gulf Stream*, shows an African-American man lying on the deck of a hurricane-battered boat and is said to have been painted in Key West by an artist who was a frequent visitor. But you got me who that was! Was he. . . ?
1. Winslow Homer
2. Grant Wood
3. James Whistler

Winslow Homer. *Who Was Who in Florida by Henry S. Marks*

Window of opportunity
An artist with his own St. Petersburg museum designed store windows for Bonwit Teller in New York in 1938—but you got me who he was! Was he. . . ?
1. Pablo Picasso
2. Georgia O'Keefe
3. Salvador Dali

Dali. And when the store rearranged his display, the Surrealist smashed the window and got himself booked for malicious mischief at the East 51st Street Police Station. *St. Petersburg Times 8-31-80*

Man of the cloth
In 1983 artist Christo draped 11 Biscayne Bay islands with pink fabric—but you got me what that art project was called! Was it. . . ?
1. *Water Hyacinths*
2. *Surrounded Islands*
3. *Silk Isles*

Surrounded Islands. In 1991 Christo dismantled his exhibit of giant 485-pound umbrellas after one of them blew over and killed a California woman. *Tampa Tribune 6-8-83 and Facts on File 10-31-91*

Others with colors

Everything you always wanted in a deer, and less

The Pulitzer prize–winning cartoonist, whose cartoon entitled "The Last of The Toy Deer" won the Pulitzer in 1943, is widely credited with kicking off the effort to save the Key deer. The national wildlife refuge on Sanibel Island is named in his honor—but you got me who he is! Is he. . . ?

1. Hank Ketchum
2. Ding Darling
3. Thomas Nast

Jay Norwood "Ding" Darling. Darling graduated from Beloit College, in Wisconsin, in 1900, which had previously kicked him out. *Tampa Tribune 9-6-64 and Encyclopedia Britannica*

Longtime Tampa resident Fred Lasswell drew the nationally known cartoon strip about Appalachian hillfolk, Snuffy Smith and his wife, Loweezy—but you got me who Snuffy and Loweezy's baby son is! Is he. . . ?

1. Tater
2. Jughead
3. Hooter

Tater. A Missouri native, Lasswell came to Gainesville at age 6 and moved to Tampa 2 years later. *Snuffy Smith* grew out of the strip *Barney Google. Tampa Tribune 10-2-77*

I'm not really bad; I'm just drawn that way

This cartoon strip character started out in 1930 as a gold digger and flapper, but her creator, Chic Young (a longtime Clearwater Beach resident), married her off to one of her suitors. But you got me who she is! Is she. . . ?

1. Blondie
2. Betty Boop
3. Mary Worth

Blondie. Chic's son, Dean Young, took over the strip upon his father's death in 1973. *Tampa Tribune 10-2-77*

God only knows

In a class of his own
The man who was the 1940 senior class president at Florida Bible Institute got some of his early training on the streets of Tampa, preaching outside saloons. But you got me who that was! Was it. . . ?
1. Billy Graham
2. Billy Sunday
3. Jimmy Swaggart

William Franklin Graham. The Bible college today is Trinity College in New Port Richey. *St. Petersburg Times 6-21-87 and 10-18-98*

You are correct, o great one
Religious visionary Cyrus Reed Teed established the settlement of New Jerusalem on the Estero River to practice the Koreshan religion, one of the central tenets of which is—you got me! Was it. . . ?
1. Whirling and singing in tongues
2. The martians are coming, the martians are coming!
3. The world is a hollow sphere, and we're all living on the inside

We all live inside the hollow world. *[www.dep.state.fl.us]*

Shut up and dance

The day the Earth stood still for Bubbles the chimp
According to Donald Trump, King of Pop/oddity Michael Jackson did something life-changing in the Tower Suite of Trump's Palm Beach estate, Mar-a-lago—but you got me what! Was it. . . ?
1. He wrote *Thriller*
2. He fell for Lisa Marie Presley
3. He had the 2nd of 3 nose jobs

He fell in love with Lisa Marie Presley (sources close to Trump question the accuracy of this). *Miami Herald [www.goflorida.com]*

It's the same old song
Stephen Foster, composer of the Florida State Song, "Old Folks at Home" (aka "Swanee River"), never visited Florida or saw the real Suwannee River. When writing the song, he came very close to using another river instead—but you got me which one! Was it. . . ?

1. Way down upon the Pee Dee River
2. Way down upon the St. Johns River
3. Way down upon the Hudson River

The Pee Dee River in the Carolinas. *St. Petersburg Times 1-12-69*

Head case
Faithful Grateful Dead fans are called Deadheads. Loyal fans of singer–songwriter Jimmy Buffett are called—you got me! Are they. . . ?
1. Margaritaheads
2. Conchheads
3. Parrotheads

Parrotheads. *The Jimmy Buffett Trivia Book by Thomas Ryan*

The English classical composer Frederick Delius (1862–1934) spent part of his youth at Solano Grove on the St. Johns near Jacksonville. One of his best-known compositions is—you got me! Is it. . . ?
1. The *Florida Suite*
2. The *Solano Symphony*
3. "Shoo fly, don't bother me"

Delius's *Florida Suite* is in 4 movements: "Day Break," "On the River," "Sunset," and "Night." In 1961 his cottage was relocated to the Jacksonville University campus. *The New Grove Dictionary of Music and Musicians and Florida Weekends by Robert Tolf and Russell Buchan*

You will be a bust, be a bust, be a bust, in the hall of fame
Born April 30, 1989, in Miami, Ellen Zwilich became the 1st woman to—you got me! Did she. . . ?
1. Fly in space
2. Win the Pulitzer prize in music
3. Marry Larry King

Zwilich won the Pulitzer in music, the 1st woman to do so. *Current Biography Yearbook 1986*

Elvis before hitting 255 lbs
When Elvis Presley appeared at St. Petersburg's Florida Theater in 1956 (the same year that TV censors kept Elvis's pelvis from the eyes

of the Ed Sullivan audience), the most expensive ticket to the show went for—you got me! Was it. . . ?

1. **$1.50**
2. **$3.25**
3. **$5.75**

$1.25 and $1.50 were the ticket prices. In 1956 the average teenager made $10.55 a week. *St. Petersburg Times 8-17-77 and Tampa Tribune 9-25-94*

BONUS Elvis question
Col. Tom Parker, the promoter who signed Elvis in 1955 and catapult-ed him to icon status, was a Tampa native who, in the 1940s, served as the city's—you got me! Was he. . . ?

1. **Dogcatcher**
2. **Fire chief**
3. **Tax collector**

Parker was Tampa's dogcatcher. *Weekly Planet May 28–June 6, 1998*

That's the way, ahuh, ahuh, I like it
In 1986 longtime Tampa area resident Frankie Yankovic won the 1st Grammy ever awarded for—you got me! Was it. . . ?

1. **Elvis impersonating**
2. **Armpit noises**
3. **Polka**

"Blue Skirt Waltz" was the signature tune of polka king Frankie Yankovic, who passed away in 1998. *AP 10-19-98*

You got me who in the Lou Reed song "Walk On the Wild Side" came from Miami, F-L-A, hitchhiked her way across the U-S-A! Was it. . . ?

1. **Viva**
2. **Holly**
3. **Little Susie**

It was Holly who said, "Hey babe, take a walk on the wild side." *"Walk On the Wild Side" lyrics*

Play it cool
Tampa native, former Ft. Lauderdale high school music teacher, and

jazz legend Julian Adderly was better known by his nickname, "Cannonball"—but you got me why he was called Cannonball! Was it because. . . ?"

1. **It evolved from Cannibal, his nickname at Florida A&M High School**
2. **He worked briefly as the Human Cannonball in The Greatest Show on Earth**
3. **He had a beer gut that looked like he'd swallowed a cannonball**

It evolved from Cannibal (he was evidentally a big eater), his nickname at Florida A&M High School. *Tampa Tribune 8-9-75*

On February 9, 1964, almost 74 million viewers, the largest audience in TV history, watched the Beatles on *The Ed Sullivan Show*, televised from the Sullivan studio on Broadway and 53rd St. in New York. The Thursday after, the Fab Four headed to Miami to do a Sunday TV show that originated from the Deauville Hotel—but you got me what show they did! Was it. . . ?

1. *The Jackie Gleason Show*
2. *The Arthur Godfrey Show*
3. *The Ed Sullivan Show*

They did another Sullivan show from the Napoleon Room at the Deauville. *A Thousand Sundays: The Story of the Ed Sullivan Show by Jerry Bowles*

In the mid-1960s Mick Jagger and Keith Richards of the Rolling Stones wrote a song in a hotel room in Clearwater Beach that became the Billboard number-one hit the week of July 10, 1965. But you got me what song! Was it...?

1. **"(I Can't Get No) Satisfaction"**
2. **"Sympathy for the Devil"**
3 **"Get Off of My Cloud"**

"Satisfaction." *The Billboard Book of Number One Hits by Fred Bronson*

Accidents happen

While touring in 1990, this Florida entertainer was seriously injured when a semi crashed into the tour bus—but you got me who that entertainer was! Was it. . . ?

1. Gloria Estefan
2. Tom Petty
3. Pat Boone

The Queen of Latin Pop, Gloria Estefan. Songs on her album "In the Light" dealt with her recovery. *AP 8-28-98*

🦜 BONUS Gloria question

Three years after her debut with the Miami Sound Machine, Gloria Estefan earned a B.A. degree from the University of Miami—but you got me what she majored in! Was it. . . ?
1. Music
2. Psychology
3. Dance

Psychology. *Current Biography Yearbook 1995*

Play that funky music, white boy

In 1955 at the Fort Homer Hesterly Armory in Tampa, Elvis Presley performed as the opening act for an entertainer who rode the music charts with a song called "What It Was Was Football." But you got me who that was! Was he. . . ?
1. Andy Griffith
2. Tennessee Ernie Ford
3. Roger Williams

Elvis opened for Andy Griffith of *Matlock* fame. *Tampa Tribune 8-17-77*

The great Ray Charles learned to play piano (and clarinet) at the St. Augustine School for the Blind. A little-known fact is that Ray changed his surname so as not to be confused with a big-time boxer of the day—but you got me what his real last name was! Was it. . . ?
1. Robinson
2. Tunney
3. Dempsey

He dropped Robinson to avoid being confused with Sugar Ray Robinson; Charles is his middle name. Ray Charles began his career playing Tampa dance halls. *Current Biography 1965 and Tampa Tribune 9-25-94*

Have a nice day

This sunny, clean-cut Jacksonville native had his *Gospel America* show dropped by a broadcasting company after he appeared at the American Music Awards in 1997 decked out in leather and a spiked dog collar—but you got me who he is! Is he singer. . . ?

1. Pat Boone
2. Wayne Newton
3. Alice Cooper

Pat Boone claimed the getup was a joke. *Current Biography 1959 and AP 9-7-98*

It's what's up front that counts

Rolling Stone magazine once showed a fake wanted poster that read: WANTED IN THE COUNTY OF DADE . . . FOR LEWD AND LASCIVIOUS BEHAVIOR IN PUBLIC. Pictured was the lead singer of the Doors—but you got me who that was! Was it. . . ?

1. Jim Morrison
2. Van Morrison
3. S/Sgt. Barry Sadler

Jim Morrison's March 1, 1969, performance at the Dinner Key auditorium got him convicted of indecent exposure and public profanity. Jackie Gleason and Anita Bryant hosted an anti-Doors decency rally at the Orange Bowl. *Light My Fire by Ray Manzarek and The Billboard Book of Number One Hits by Fred Bronson*

When you least expect it, you're elected

Government of laws, not men

In 1978 Governor Reubin Askew appointed the state's 1st woman state attorney. But you got me who it was! Was she. . . ?

1. Janet Vegas
2. Janet Reno
3. Janet Tahoe

Miami native Janet Reno went on to become Attorney General in the Clinton administration. *Tampa Tribune 1-5-78*

The 27th person accorded the honor of lying in state in the Capitol Rotunda was the oldest member of Congress at the time of his death, and a champion of elderly rights—but you got me who he was! Was he. . . ?

1. Claude Pepper
2. Sam Gibbons
3. Tip O'Neill

Claude Pepper, 88, died May 30, 1989. *Facts on File 6-2-89*

Sugar daddy

The Pennsuco Sugar Company sent Ernest "Cap" Graham to Florida in 1921 to drain the swamps and plant sugarcane. Wiped out by a 1926 hurricane, Graham turned to farming. One of his sons was Philip Graham, former publisher of the *Washington Post*. (Katharine Graham succeeded her husband as president of the Washington Post Company upon his suicide in 1963.) His youngest son Bob is—you got me! Is he...?

1. **The current *Washington Post* publisher**
2. **A senator from Florida**
3. **The inventor of Nutrasweet**

Elected in 1986, Bob Graham served as the senior senator from Florida. He also served as the state's 38th governor from 1978–1986. *Encyclopedia Britannica, [www.senate.gov], and [www.floridacrystals.com]*

Business as usual

Jeff Bezos grew up in the Kendall section of Miami and founded a cyberspace business empire that went online in July 1995—but you got me what Internet business he started up! Is it...?

1. **Amazon.com**
2. **America Online**
3. **Yahoo!**

Bookseller Amazon.com operates out of Seattle. *St. Petersburg Times 9-22-98*

This Green Cove Springs native brought Wall Street to Main Street with his pioneering work in the field of selling stocks and bonds to small investors—but you got me who he was! Was he...?

1. **Charles Merrill of Merrill Lynch**
2. **Dean Witter**
3. **Charles Schwab**

Charles Edward Merrill was born October 19, 1885. *Current Biography 1956*

Land grab

It's estimated that this Coral Gables winter resident purchased one-fifth of Dade County. But you got me who he was! Was he. . . ?

1. **Arthur Vining Davis (Alcoa chairman)**
2. **Joe Robbie (original Dolphins owner)**
3. **Wayne Huizenga (waste/video/sports magnate)**

Arthur Vining Davis (1887–1962). *Who Was Who in Florida by Henry S. Marks*

Keep on truckin'

In 1933 a Miami construction worker put $35 down on a Model-A Ford truck. Over the next 45 years, he built up the largest truck-leasing company in the nation. But you got me who he is! Is he. . . ?

1. **Ryder**
2. **Mack**
3. **Hertz**

James Ryder. *Forbes 4-3-89*

Got milk?

One well-known cookie entrepreneur grew up on East Lafayette Street in Tallahassee, in the shadow of the Capitol—but you got me who! Was it. . . ?

1. **Mrs. Fields**
2. **Famous Amos**
3. **David of David's Cookies**

Wally "Famous" Amos. *St. Petersburg Times 3-18-83*

Who all

Haven't I seen you somewhere before?

Retired schoolteacher Anne Turner Cook of Tampa served as the model for a well-known character seen on a commercial product—but you got me whom she was the model for! Was it. . . ?

1. **The Gerber baby**
2. **Betty Crocker**
3. **Aunt Jemima**

As an infant, she was the model for the Gerber baby. *Anne Turner Cook personal interview*

America's most famous treasure hunter, Mel Fisher (d. 12-19-98)

trained as a hydraulic engineer at Purdue and then went into business
with his father—but you got me what kind of business! Was it. . . ?

    1. Electronics
    2. Farming
    3. Insurance

**Poultry farming. After 4 years he unloaded the business and opened
a dive shop in Redondo Beach, California. Fisher discovered the
Atocha, which took its treasure to the bottom off the Keys in a 1622
hurricane. *Tampa Tribune 11-3-75***

🪝 BONUS shipwreck question

The earliest shipwreck of a slave ship identified by name in the
Western Hemisphere sank in 1700 west of Key West after unloading
190 slaves in Jamaica. But you got me what the name of that slaver
was! Was it. . . ?

    1. *Henrietta Marie*
    2. *Golden Ibis*
    3. *Queen Isabella*

**The English slaver *Henrietta Marie* was found by a subsidiary group
of Mel Fisher in 1972. [www.melfisher.org]**

Dr. Gilbert H. Grosvenor, Coconut Grove winter resident, edited from
1900 to 1954 the magazine that was one of the 1st to show color
photos—but you got me what mag! Was it. . . ?

    1. *Good Housekeeping*
    2. *Life*
    3. *National Geographic*

**Under Grosvenor, *National Geographic*'s circulation grew from 900 to
1,900,000. *Encyclopedia Britannica and St. Petersburg Times 1-12-48***

Check it out

Someone who sprang into the public eye spent the night of
December 6, 1980, checked in at Room 538 at the Sheraton Sand Key
Resort in Clearwater Beach—but you got me who! Was it. . . ?

    1. **Mark David Chapman, 2 nights before he killed John Lennon**
    2. **Jessica Hahn, for her liaison with PTL evangelist Jim Bakker**
    3. **Jimi Hendrix, the night he was found dead**

Jessica Hahn. *Forgiven by Charles E. Shepard*

Tropical Chachka

In 1957 a man named Don Featherstone created this classic piece of kitsch as a tribute to Florida's "tropical splendor." But you got me what! Was it. . . ?

1. The official Florida license plate
2. The pink flamingo lawn ornament
3. The Florida snowdome

The pink flamingo lawn ornament. *St. Petersburg Times 5-6-98*

Would you like a booth?

On July 13, 1971, 20-year-old Rhonda Spence stepped into a booth in DeFuniak Springs and became the 1st person in Florida to—you got me! Was it. . . ?

1. Desegregate Florida lunch counters
2. Cast a vote under the age of 21
3. Place a phone call to space

Spence was the 1st under-21 to cast a vote in Florida. *Florida Handbook 1997–1998*

It's the thought that counts

In 1951 when legendary Palm Beach socialite and former Versailles nightclub cigarette girl, Brownie McLean, married mining squillionaire, Jock McLean (whose family once owned the *Washington Post*), Jock offered her a wedding gift that Brownie turned down because she believed the thing was cursed—but you got me what! Was it. . . ?

1. The Hope Diamond
2. The Gold Mask of Tutankhamen
3. The Maltese Falcon

The Hope Diamond. *Palm Beach Babylon by Murray Weiss and Bill Hoffmann*

Naturalist and explorer William Bartram (son of John "Father of American Botany" Bartram) wrote *Travels* (1791), which served as the inspiration for one poet's famous vision of Xanadu, where Kubla Khan a stately pleasure dome decreed and where a sacred river ran through caverns measureless to man—but you got me what poet! Was it. . . ?

1. Henry Wadsworth Longfellow
2. Samuel Taylor Coleridge
3. John Keats

Coleridge wrote *Kubla Khan*. *Some Kind of Paradise by Mark Derr*

It was a cry for help
One of the famed "barefoot mailmen," a 6'7" giant named James "Acrefoot" Johnson, quit the mail game when the postal service refused to let him carry something on his route—but you got me what! Was it. . . ?
1. Whiskey for snakebites
2. Weapons
3. A passenger

Johnson wanted to carry passengers on his back; the Palm Beach–Miami route was a 6-day round-trip. *Florida Trend Oct 83*

It's better to have loved and won
After winning a quick acquittal in the 1991 rape trial of William Kennedy Smith, high-profile defense lawyer Roy Black met and married—you got me! Did he marry. . . ?
1. The William Kennedy Smith trial judge
2. A William Kennedy Smith trial juror
3. The alleged William Kennedy Smith victim

On the night of the verdict, Roy Black, in a bar, ran into one of the jurors that had acquitted his client, and they were later married. *[www.abcnews.com]*

Vincente Martinez Ybor, Spanish bigwig in Cuba, moved his business (in the face of labor unrest) first to Key West in 1869 and then to Tampa in 1885. But you got me what kind of business Ybor had! Was it. . . ?
1. Citrus, principally grapefruit
2. Cigar
3. Phosphate mining

Cigar. Tampa and Ybor City (envisioned as a company town for the workers) supported 120 cigar factories by 1896 and by 1920 employed 12,000. *Weekly Planet June 11–17, 1998*

If you're gonna bump it

After a scandalous divorce trial from Herbert "Peter" Pultizer, Palm Beach socialite Roxanne Pulitzer was branded with the humorous nickname—you got me! Was she known as. . . ?

1. "The strumpet with a trumpet"
2. "The jellybean queen"
3. "The chippy in the chips"

Roxanne Pulitzer became known as "the strumpet with a trumpet" and posed for the June 1985 issue of *Playboy. The Prize Pulitzer by Roxanne Pulitzer*

The world before Slurpees

Apalachicola resident John Gorrie was granted the 1st U.S. patent for mechanical refrigeration in 1851 and is considered the founder of air conditioning—but you got me what his occupation was! Was he a. . . ?

1. Physician
2. Lawyer
3. Fisherman

As a physician, Gorrie was attempting to help his yellow-fever patients by cooling hospital rooms. His invention received British patent #13,234 in August 1850 and U.S. patent #8080, issued May 6, 1851. *Encyclopedia Britannica and Lost Pages from American History by Webb Garrison*

Her heart (and most of everything else) belonged to Daddy

The grand dame of Palm Beach society was for many years Marjorie Merriweather Post, cereal heiress who got her money from her father, Charles William Post. Mr. Post, before breaking through with the beverage Postum, invented a blade that made him big bucks—but you got me what kind of blade! Was it a. . . ?

1. Plow blade
2. Razor blade
3. Airplane propeller blade

He invented a blade for the common plow. *Tampa Tribune 12-15-68*

There she is

Tampa's Margaret "Mickey" Ekdahl came in 3rd in the Miss America pageant of 1930 but stepped into the title when both the winner and the 1st runner-up were disqualified! But you got me how come the top 2 got the boot? Was it. . . ?

1. **They were unmasked as communists**
2. **One was married; the other didn't come from the state on her sash**
3. **They got into an ugly catfight afterward**

The winner was married and the runner-up didn't come from or live in her state. Miss America 1999 was a Florida native and USF grad but competed as Miss Virginia. *St. Petersburg Times 9-10-80 and 9-20-98 and Facts on File 9-24-92*

🐟 BONUS beauty pageant question

On May 16, 1997, in Miami Beach, Brook Lee was crowned the new Miss Universe. But you got me what country she hailed from! Was it. . . ?

1. **Trinidad and Tobago**
2. **Australia**
3. **U.S.**

Brook Lee of Hawaii was the 7th Miss Universe from the U.S. *[www.missuniverse.com]*

Mon dieu

Napoleon's nephew, Prince Achille Murat (1801–1847), settled on a Tallahassee plantation and was married to the great-grandniece of one of our founding fathers. But you got me who! Was it. . . ?

1. **Ben Franklin**
2. **Thomas Jefferson**
3. **George Washington**

 Madame Catharine Murat (1803–1867) was Washington's great-grandniece. *Who Was Who in Florida by Henry S. Marks*

Chapter 15

Hail to the Chief—
Presidents in Florida

And I believe for every drop of rain that falls a flower grows

Standing near the monorail at Disney World in November 1973, President Richard Nixon, addressing editors from 43 states, said—you got me! Was it. . . ?

1. "I'm not a crook"
2. "You won't have Nixon to kick around anymore"
3. "When the President does it, that means that it is not illegal"

The quote was, " . . . people have got to know whether or not their President is a crook. Well, I'm not a crook. I earned everything I got." *Chronicle of America*

Party animal

Warren Harding vacationed at the Flamingo Hotel in Miami Beach before his March 4, 1921, inauguration. In a famous photo op, the President-elect played golf with a caddy named Carl II. But you got me what Carl was! Was he. . . ?

1. A chimp
2. A baby elephant
3. A donkey

Carl II (later Nero) was a baby elephant. *Florida's Promoters by Charles E. Horner*

On March 4, 1997, President Bill Clinton was hospitalized in West Palm Beach after an unfortunate incident at the home of golfer Greg Norman—but you got me what! Was it. . . ?

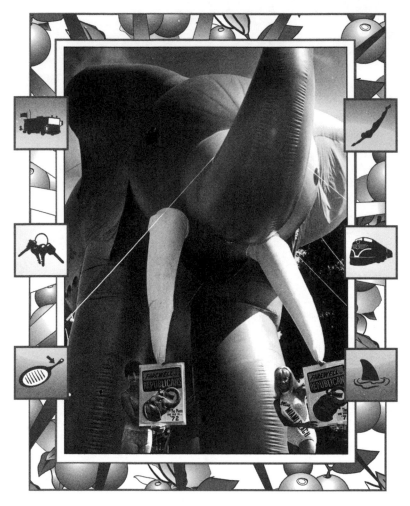

The Citrus Queen and Miss Miami Beach with the Florida Citrus Commission balloon at the Republican National Convention, Miami, 1968

1. President Clinton fell asleep in the hot tub
2. Norman shanked one and beaned the President
3. The President tumbled down some steps

President Bill Clinton tumbled down some steps. *Morning Edition (NPR) 3-14-97*

In the 1980, 1984, and 1988 presidential elections, Florida went Republican (for Reagan twice and then Bush). But you got me which way the state went in 1992! Was it for. . . ?
1. George Bush
2. Bill Clinton
3. Ross Perot

Florida went for Bush, but only by the narrow margin of about 100,000 votes (40.9% to Clinton's 39%); Perot didn't figure. *Florida Handbook 1997–1998*

The buck stops in Florida

The 2-story frame house from 1891 (6 bd/5 ba) that served as President Truman's "Little White House" was built on a Naval base as a home for the base commander—but you got me where it was! Was it. . . ?
1. Key West
2. Key Biscayne
3. Pensacola

Key West. *Tampa Sunday Tribune 12-2-51 and Holiday Dec 1949*

In 1972 both the Republicans and the Democrats held their national conventions in Miami Beach. The Republicans renominated Richard Nixon—but you got me who the Democrats tapped! Was it. . . ?
1. Hubert Humphrey
2. George McGovern
3. Edward Muskie

McGovern was nominated July 10th in Miami Beach; Nixon's 1968 nomination also came in Miami Beach. *Information Please Almanac 1995*

In 1929 one U.S. president made his final address as chief executive when he dedicated Edward Bok's famous Singing Tower—but you got me what president! Was it. . . ?

1. Woodrow Wilson
2. Herbert Hoover
3. Calvin Coolidge

Coolidge, who once said, "I think the people of America want a solemn ass for president and I do not want to disappoint them." *Tampa Tribune 2-1-79 and AP 8-12-98*

Size matters
On December 6, 1947, when President Truman was on hand for the dedication of Everglades National Park, the park was the 28th in the national park system, and, in terms of size, it was—you got me! Was it. . . ?
1. The biggest in the nation
2. Second biggest
3. Third

At 454,000 acres, it ranked third behind Yellowstone (2,213,000 acres) and Mt. McKinley National Park in Alaska (1,939,199 acres). *Tampa Tribune 12-7-47*

On the boards
Strapped to a board after back surgery, at his father's house in Palm Beach, JFK did something that gained him national attention—but you got me what! Was it. . . ?
1. Wrote his Pulitzer prize–winning *Profiles in Courage*
2. Faced down Khrushchev during the Cuban missile crisis
3. Wed Jackie

He wrote *Profiles in Courage* while strapped to a board. *Encyclopedia Britannica*

This class ad ran in *The New York Law Journal*: FORMER PRESIDENT'S HISTORIC KEY BISCAYNE "FLORIDA WHITE HOUSE." PRESIDENTIAL COMPOUND ESTATE-RETREAT. PRESIDENTIAL LIBRARY FOR CONFERENCES. MAGNIFICENT SITE. 265' WATERFRONT, PRIVATE BEACH, LUXURIANT GROUNDS. FOR SALE, $685,000, OR RENT WEEKLY OR MONTHLY WITH MAID SERVICE. CHEF-CHAUFFEUR OPTIONAL. But you got me which President's place that was! Was it. . . ?
1. John F. Kennedy's
2. Richard Nixon's
3. Gerald Ford's

Nixon's. *Tampa Tribune 10-2-76*

You got me which U.S. president was the first to overnight at the Florida Capitol in the 20th century! Was it. . . ?
1. Teddy Roosevelt
2. John F. Kennedy
3. Jimmy Carter

Carter stayed over on October 9, 1980. *Florida Handbook 1997–1998*

In deep water
President LBJ kicked off construction on the Cross-Florida Barge Canal in 1964—but you got me which president pulled the plug on the controversial waterway! Was it. . . ?
1. Nixon, in 1971
2. Reagan, in 1981
3. Clinton, in 1991

Nixon did, 6 years before the scheduled completion date. *Florida Handbook 1997–1998*

One U.S. president spent the last weekend of his life in the state of Florida—but you got me who! Was it. . . ?
1. Andrew Jackson
2. Theodore Roosevelt
3. John F. Kennedy

President Kennedy was assassinated on Friday, November 22, 1963. The previous weekend was spent at the Kennedy winter home in Palm Beach. *Tampa Tribune 11-8-63*

⚓ BONUS JFK question
His last Monday alive, JFK flew to Tampa from West Palm Beach to speak at Al Lopez Field in commemoration of the 50th anniversary of—you got me! Was it. . . ?
1. His parents' wedding
2. The birth of commercial aviation
3. The end of World War I

The birth of commercial aviation. *AP 11-8-63*

Character assassination
On the night of February 15, 1933, an unemployed bricklayer (and probable nutjob) named Guiseppe Zangara assassinated Chicago

mayor Anton Cermak in Bayfront Park, Miami. But you got me for whom Zangara was really gunning! Was it. . . ?
1. **Al Capone**
2. **FDR**
3. **José Martí**

Zangara was trying to assassinate President-elect Franklin D. Roosevelt. He was electrocuted at Raiford on March 20th, 2 quick weeks after Cermak died. Reportedly his last words to the sheriff/executioner were "Pusha da button." *Yesterday's Miami by Nixon Smiley*

Friends in high places

In 1962, when Richard Nixon lost his bid for governor of California and announced his retirement from politics ("You won't have Nixon to kick around anymore"), a Tampa-born businessman arranged for Nixon to pick up a piece of undeveloped Fisher Island in Biscayne Bay. But you got me who that Nixon friend and confidant was! Was he. . . ?
1. **Bebe Rebozo**
2. **H. R. Haldeman**
3. **John Erlichman**

Charles Gregory (Bebe) Rebozo. *Tampa Tribune 12-24-68*

In the 1976 presidential election, Jimmy Carter carried 24 states, including Florida, and the District of Columbia. But you got me who got Florida's 17 electoral votes in 1980! Was it. . . ?
1. **Jimmy Carter**
2. **Ronald Reagan**
3. **Gerald Ford**

Ronald Reagan. Carter carried only 6 states and D.C. in 1980. *St. Petersburg Times 11-6-80*

One legendary story goes that before he signed the Cuban trade embargo, President Kennedy ordered Press Secretary Pierre Salinger to go out and buy him something—but you got me what! Was it. . . ?
1. **A bulletproof vest**
2. **Cigars**
3. **A 50-lb. bag of Cuban sugar**

Salinger supposedly bought 1,200 H. Upmann Petit Coronas, Kennedy's favorite cigar, before the embargo went into effect. *[www.cigaraficionado.com]*

On March 13, 1904, President Teddy Roosevelt issued an executive order establishing the nation's 1st National Wildlife Refuge—but you got me what it was! Was it. . . ?
  1. Pelican Island
  2. Flamingo Key
  3. Corkscrew Swamp

Pelican Island. In 1908 he created the Ocala National Forest, the only national forest east of the Mississippi. *St. Petersburg Times 9-20-83, AP 11-25-83, and Frommer's Florida '94*

Better known as a hero of the Mexican War (1846–48), in 1837 the future 12th president of the U.S. was promoted to brigadier general for his leadership at the Battle of Lake Okeechobee during the Second Seminole War—but you got me who he was! Was he. . . ?
  1. Andrew Jackson
  2. Zachary Taylor
  3. Ulysses S. Grant

Zachary Taylor lead the 3-hour, Christmas Day battle; he passed away 16 months after taking the office of president. *Florida's Past by Gene M. Burnett and Encyclopedia Britannica*

And one wannabe President
Before the 1988 presidential election, the *National Enquirer* published a photo of Democratic hopeful Gary Hart with a woman other than his wife perched on his knee. The woman was Donna Rice. But you got me what the name of the boat was on which they'd been cavorting! Was it. . . ?
  1. *True Love*
  2. *Monkey Business*
  3. *Bimbo II*

 Monkey Business was the boat. *National Enquirer 9-29-98*

YOU GOT ME...

Gymnasts at Florida State University, Tallahassee, 1953

Chapter 16
We Will, We Will Rock You—Florida Sports

A Yakhoob by any other name
When Minneapolis attorney Joe Robbie was awarded the AFL's 1st expansion franchise, he enlisted the backing of the entertainer who founded St. Jude's Hospital and was born with the name Muzyad Yakhoob—but you got who that was! Was it. . . ?
1. Danny Thomas
2. Jimmy Durante
3. Al Jolson

Although his parents changed it to Amos Jacobs, he was better known as Danny Thomas. *Total Football: The Official Encyclopedia of the NFL and Annual Obituary 1991*

🏈 BONUS Joe Robbie question
Although Joe Robbie lived part-time in Miami when he was awarded the franchise for the team that would become the Dolphins, Miami wasn't his 1st choice—but you got me what city he wanted to put his team in instead! Was it. . . ?
1. Houston
2. Philadelphia
3. Jacksonville

Philadelphia. *Total Football: The Official Encyclopedia of the NFL*

In the decade from 1986 to 1996, you got me how many times the Heisman Trophy was won by quarterbacks at Florida schools! Was it. . . ?
1. Twice
2. Three times
3. Four times

Testaverde (UM) in 1986, Toretta (UM) in 1992, Ward (FSU) in 1993, and Wuerffel (UF) in 1996. The only previous Florida winner was Steve Spurrier (UF) in 1966, today head coach at UF. *[www.college-football.org]*

One strike, you're out

Lightning deaths are associated with one sport more than any other—but you got me what sport! Is it. . . ?
1. Swimming
2. Golfing
3. Baseball

Golfers make up 7% of lightning deaths. *Florida Weather by Morton D. Winsberg*

Playing the field

In 1901, when Florida Agricultural College (later UF) played its 1st football game ever against Stetson, players had to contend with something on the edge of the field that interfered with play—but you got me what! Was it a. . . ?
1. Stump
2. Rattlesnake
3. Sinkhole

The game was played at the fairgrounds in Jacksonville, and there was a tree stump on the field. *Go Gators! Official History of University of Florida Football 1889–1967*

In 1959 this baseball manager and Ybor City native was responsible for guiding his team, the Chicago "Go-Go" White Sox, to its 1st pennant in 40 years, beating the Yankees, no less! But you got me who this Hall of Famer is! Is he. . . ?
1. Al Lopez
2. Lou Boudreau
3. Casey Stengel

Al Lopez. *Current Biography 1960*

Before Super Bowl III at the Orange Bowl, this Jets quarterback "guaranteed" a victory over the Colts. But you got me who that was! Was he. . . ?

1. Roger Staubach
2. Fran Tarkenton
3. Joe Namath

Broadway Joe Namath guaranteed it, and on January 12, 1969, the Jets won 16–7. *Encyclopedia Britannica and Information Please Almanac*

Halloween 1998, the Orlando Magic introduced its mascot to the world at Church Street Station—but you got me who the mascot is! Is it. . . ?
1. **Stuff the Magic Dragon**
2. **Touché the Magic Touch**
3. **Merlin the Magician**

Stuff is the Magic's mascot; Dave Raymond was in the suit that 1st night. *Making Magic: How Orlando Won an NBA Team by Pat Williams with Larry Guest*

Cassius Clay (before he became Muhammad Ali) won the world heavyweight title when Sonny Liston failed to answer the bell for the 7th round at Miami Beach's Convention Hall. The Miami Boxing Commission fined Clay $2,500 for doing something at the weigh-in— but you got me what! Was he fined for. . . ?
1. **Sucker-punching Liston**
2. **Yelling and jumping around**
3. **Showing up late**

Clay (who made an est. $600K for the fight) was fined for yelling and jumping around. Ybor City native Ferdie Pacheco later rose to national- al prominence as Ali's ringside doctor. *Facts on File 2-20-64 to 2-26-64 and Tampa Tribune 9-25-94*

In his professional debut, this golfer, known as the Golden Bear, lost an exhibition match in Miami in 1961 to Gary Player—but you got me who he is! Is he. . . ?
1. **Arnold Palmer**
2. **Jack Nicklaus**
3. **Tom Watson**

Jack Nicklaus, who beat Palmer in an 18-hole playoff to win his 1st major, the U.S. Open, in 1962. *Current Biography 1962*

No price is too great for nacho cheese sauce
You got me how much fans spend on average for concessions at Pro Player Stadium (formerly Joe Robbie Stadium), where the Marlins and Dolphins play! Is it. . . ?
1. $5.50
2. $10
3. $22

$10, with about 40% of that going to the team. *New York Times Magazine 10-18-98*

Trouble with a capital T
The 1st time this game was played in the U.S. was in 1565, in St. Augustine. But you got me what game! Was it. . . ?
1. Billiards
2. Baseball
3. Golf

Billiards. *Florida Handbook 1997–1998*

According to the July 14, 1892, *Tropical Sun*, the 1st of these games in the Biscayne Bay area was played 1½ miles out of Lemon City—but you got me what game! Was it. . . ?
1. Soccer
2. Baseball
3. Football

Baseball. FYI: Abner Doubleday, who according to legend invented the game in 1839, served as a captain at Fort Dallas (today's Miami). *South Florida History Magazine Winter 1993*

Stupid pet tricks
When the Miami Dolphins began play at the Orange Bowl in 1966, each and every time they scored a touchdown something happened—but you got me what! Was it. . . ?
1. Flamingoes were released into the air
2. A dolphin performed a leap
3. Don Shula's pet bulldog ran the length of the field

A dolphin from the TV show *Flipper* did leaps. *Historical Traveler's Guide to Florida by Eliot Kleinberg*

On September 23, 1992, Manon Rheaume became the 1st woman to play in one of the 4 major North American sports. But you got me what sport! Was it. . . ?

   1. Baseball
   2. Hockey
   3. Basketball

Goaltender Rheaume played the 1st period in the preseason when hockey's St. Louis Blues played the Tampa Bay Lightning. *Tampa Tribune 5-19-98*

Hit happens

On April 4, 1919, in Tampa, this slugger smacked his longest home run: 587 feet. But you got me who! Was it. . . ?

   1. Babe Ruth
   2. Ty Cobb
   3. Shoeless Joe Jackson

Babe Ruth, in the preseason for the Boston Red Sox. *Baseball in Florida by Kevin M. McCarthy*

At the old ball game

Known as "the voice of Brooklyn" for his Dodgers coverage, this baseball commentator got his 1st break in radio announcing on the University of Florida station, WRUF—but you got me who this colorful character was! Was he. . . ?

   1. Red Barber
   2. Mel Allen
   3. Vin Scully

Born in Mississippi, Red Barber (d. 1993) moved to the Sanford area at age 10. *Current Biography 1943 and 1993*

Debuting in 1998, the Tampa Bay Devil Rays got their 1st win April 1st when they defeated—you got me! Was it. . . ?

   1. The Detroit Tigers
   2. The New York Mets
   3. The Los Angeles Dodgers

They beat the Tigers 11–8. *Facts on File 4-16-98*

A good sport
One sport made its U.S. professional debut in Miami in 1935—but you got me which one! Was it. . . ?
1. Soccer
2. Jai alai
3. Shuffleboard

Jai alai, which means "merry festival" in Basque. The sport was 1st seen in the U.S. at the St. Louis World's Fair in 1904. *Florida Handbook 1997–1998 and New York Times 3-16-75*

On June 9, 1996, long-distance swimmer Susie Maroney set a world record when she swam 88.5 miles and crossed into U.S. waters 10 miles shy of Key West. But you got me where she started from! Was it. . . ?
1. Havana
2. Grand Bahama
3. San Juan

Maroney started out June 8th from Havana and swam 36 hours, part of the way in a shark cage. *Facts on File 6-27-96*

No-win situation
You got me how many NFL games the Tampa Bay Buccaneers lost before finally winning one! Was it. . . ?
1. They won the very first game they played
2. They lost 8 in a row
3. They lost 26

Awarded the 27th NFL franchise on April 24, 1974, the Bucs began play in 1976. They went 0–26 (the 2nd longest losing streak in NFL history, behind the Chicago Cardinals's 29-game streak) before beating the New Orleans Saints in December 1977. *Tampa Tribune 12-12-77*

You had to be there
January 1, 1996, was the last time you could have seen something at the Orange Bowl in Miami—but you got me what! Was it. . . ?
1. The Orange Bowl Game
2. A visit by Pope John Paul II
3. Packy the Wombat, former mascot of UM

The Orange Bowl Game. *Historical Traveler's Guide to Florida by Eliot Kleinberg*

Putting on the dog

Derby Lane Greyhound Park in St. Petersburg is the nation's oldest dog track, but Hialeah boasts the state's 1st electrical—you got me! Was it. . . ?

1. Lights
2. Paramutuel betting
3. Rabbit

The electrical "rabbit," invented by O. P. Smith in 1919. Legal in 18 states, almost one-third of all dog tracks are in Florida. *Florida Handbook 1997–1998 and Harper's Magazine 2-99*

During the 1987 season, the UM Hurricanes went undefeated and won the National Championship. In 1988 the 'Canes lost 1 game only and lost it by only 1 point—but you got me to whom they lost! Was it. . . ?

1. Penn State
2. Notre Dame
3. Nebraska

Notre Dame. *Hurricanes Handbook by Jim Martz*

In 1906, in the University of Florida's 1st football game, the Gators met Stetson on the gridiron. But you got me who won! Was it. . . ?

1. UF 6–0
2. Stetson 27–7
3. They tied 14-all.

Florida took the game 6–0 over Stetson. Earlier football games were played by Florida Agricultural College at Lake City before it was relocated to Gainesville as UF. *Go Gators! The Official History of University of Florida Football 1889–1906*

Sign of the times

Babe Ruth supposedly signed his 1st baseball contract in the lobby of the Tampa Bay Hotel (now the University of Tampa) as a left-handed pitcher for—you got me! Was it. . . ?

1. The New York Yankees
2. The Brooklyn Dodgers
3. The Boston Red Sox

The Bambino signed with the Boston Red Sox, of the American League, in 1914; he became an outfielder for the Yankees in 1920. *The University of Tampa Foundation 1966 and Encyclopedia Britannica*

The heavyweight champ who took the title away from "Jersey" Joe Walcott in 1952 and became the 2nd person to knock out Joe Louis died in a plane crash in Des Moines and was laid to rest at Lauderdale Memorial Gardens in Fort Lauderdale—but you got me who he was! Was he. . . ?
    1. Rocky Marciano
    2. Jake LaMotta
    3. Billy Graham

Rocco Francis Marchegiano, aka Rocky Marciano. *Final Placement by Robert B. Dickerson Jr.*

In 1984 Tampa hosted the USFL (United States Football League) title game on July 15th. That same year Tampa hosted another big sporting event—but you got me what! Was it. . . ?
    1. The Super Bowl
    2. The P.G.A. Championship
    3. The 1984 Summer Olympics

On January 22, 1984, Super Bowl XVIII (Raiders vs. Redskins) was played at Tampa Stadium. *Tampa Tribune 10-20-83*

Here comes the judge
In 1912 the entire football team of the University of Florida, in Cuba to play a couple of games during the Christmas holidays, was rounded up by police and headed off to municipal court—but you got me what they did! Did they. . . ?
    1. Have a kegger
    2. Forfeit the game
    3. Skinny-dip

Believing the ref biased (he was the Cuban team's former coach), the team walked off the field and forfeited the game, which a local statute prohibited at events with paying spectators. *Tampa Tribune 9-9-73*

Of its 9 games in the year 1946, you got me how many the Florida Gators lost! Was it. . . ?

1. 0
2. 1
3. 9

They lost all 9, plus the 1st 4 games of 1947, for the longest losing streak in Gator history. *Tampa Tribune-Times 7-21-74*

The very 1st Orange Bowl game was played in 1933, with Manhattan College going down in defeat to the local team—but you got me who that was! Was it. . . ?
1. **Florida State**
2. **University of Florida**
3. **University of Miami**

University of Miami. *Yesterday's Miami by Nixon Smiley*

Pleased as punch
Muhammad Ali claimed to have won the Heavyweight Championship in 1965 by using a secret punch taught to him by early screen legend and Key West native Stepin Fetchit—but you got me who was on the receiving end of that punch! Was it. . . ?
1. **Sonny Liston**
2. **Joe Frazier**
3. **Ernie Terrell**

Sonny Liston. Fetchit claimed he'd learned the punch from fighter Jack Johnson. *Whatever Became Of. . . ? (8th series)*

What a "female canine animal, especially a dog!"
At a dog track, where the greyhounds can hit 40 mph, the dogs are—you got me! Are they. . . ?
1. **Males, because they're stronger**
2. **Females, because they're faster**
3. **Both males and females**

Without regard to sex, male and female dogs race. *The Wall Street Journal 12-22-74*

On April 1, 1959, U.S. District Court judge Bryan Simpson ordered complete desegregation of Jacksonville's—you got me! Was it. . . ?
1. **Little League**
2. **Public transportation**
3. **Golf courses**

Until that time, African-Americans were permitted to play on one of the 2 city-owned golf courses on Mondays only, and the other on Fridays. In response, the city commissioners shut them both down. *UPI 4-2-59 and AP 4-3-59*

Three-time Presidential loser and prosecutor at the Scopes Monkey Trial, William Jennings Bryan once campaigned against gambling for fear it would ruin a particular sport—but you got me what sport Bryan wanted to save from the evils of gambling! Was it. . . ?
1. Thoroughbred racing
2. Greyhound racing
3. Jai alai

Jai alai. *New York Times 3-16-75*

Dream team
The youngest franchise in the history of major league baseball to win the World Series was—you got me! Was it. . . ?
1. The Florida Marlins
2. The Tampa Bay Devil Rays
3. The Jacksonville Jaguars

In 1997 the Cleveland Indians went down to the Marlins, playing in only their 5th season. The Jaguars play football. *Miami Herald 10-27-97 [www.sportspapers.com]*

In 1928 Dick "The Father of Florida Tourism" Pope, at Miami Beach, became the 1st person in the world to do something on water skis—but you got me what! Was it. . . ?
1. Do ballet
2. Flip
3. Jump over a ramp

Pope, the founder of Cypress Gardens, skied over a wooden ramp, travelling 25 feet. *Tampa Tribune 6-29-58*

Delay of game
In 1992 the Miami Dolphins postponed their September 6th home opener against the New England Patriots because of—you got me! Was it. . . ?

1. A hurricane
2. A players' strike
3. Thousands of counterfeit tickets

The game was put off in the wake of Hurricane Andrew, which blew through there August 24, 1992. *Palm Beach Post 9-21-92*

BONUS Dolphins question

In 1997 the coach of the Miami Dolphins retired with more career wins than any other coach. But you got me who he was! Was he. . . ?
1. Jimmy Johnson
2. Don Shula
3. Mike Ditka

Don Shula won 347 games, plus 2 Super Bowl championships. When Shula retired, Jimmy Johnson took over the reins. *1997 People Entertainment Almanac*

The very rich are different from you and me

A retired multimillionaire at age 45, Wayne Huizenga went on to turn Blockbuster into the largest video chain in the nation, as well as purchasing ownership stakes in 3 professional teams—the Marlins, the Dolphins, and the Panthers. But you got me what business Huizenga made his 1st million in! Was it. . . ?
1. Chain restaurants
2. Garbage
3. Software

Huizenga started out driving a garbage truck and built his Waste Management company into the largest of its kind in the world. *Public and Private Coalitions by Larry Glasser [charlotte.acns.nwu.edu]*

Race relations

The inaugural Daytona 500, in 1959, was won with an average speed of around 135 mph by a member of one of racing's 1st families—but you got me what family! Was it. . . ?
1. Petty
2. Andretti
3. Earnhardt

Lee Petty took the 1st Daytona 500 in 1959; his son Richard was Rookie of the Year. *St. Petersburg Times 2-13-98*

BONUS Speedway question

You got me how many fatalities occurred at the Daytona International Speedway between its opening in 1959 and March 1994! Was it. . . ?

1. Only 1
2. 7
3. 25

The death of NASCAR driver Neil Bonnett on February 11, 1994, the most recent as of this writing, brought the number to 25. *Facts on File 3-10-94*

Chapter 17

Been There, Done That—Tourist Florida

The happiest place on Earth: Disney World

A fairy-tale character's home is his castle
One of the towers of Cinderella's Castle at Disney World houses a special apartment—but you got me for whom it was built! Was it. . . ?
1. The Disney family
2. The cryonically frozen remains of Walt
3. Disney CEO Michael Eisner

The Disney Family, though it was reportedly never used. *Birnbaum's Walt Disney World 1998*

In 1998 Disney lobbying efforts paid off when it won an extension on the copyright on Mickey Mouse, which was set to expire in 2003. But you got me what the new expiration date on Mickey is! Is it. . . ?
1. 2023
2. 2053
3. Never

Disney won a 20-year extension. Pluto, Goofy, and Donald Duck enter the public domain in 2025, 2027, and 2029 respectively. *AP 10-17-98*

Disney World opened to the public in October 1971. But you got me how many people visited it in its 1st year! Was it. . . ?
1. Almost 2 million
2. Almost 7 million
3. Almost 11 million

Almost 11 million. In its 1st 11 years, 140 million. *Tampa Tribune 9-28-71 and 10-1-82*

The dustbin of history

POST CARD

Having a
Marvelous Time —

Opening night dance at the tin can tourist convention, Arcadia, 1950

When Disney World first opened, you got me how much trash the average visitor disposed of during a day in the park! Was it. . . ?
1. **About ½ pound**
2. **1 to 1½ pounds**
3. **6 to 7 pounds**

1 to 1½ pounds. 1989 stats put that number at 90 tons of trash daily. *Tampa Times 1-21-72 and Reedy Creek Energy Services, 1989*

🐾 BONUS early Disney question
On opening day at Disney World (1971), one monorail pilot was grounded because of something to do with her underwear—but you got me what! Was it. . . ?
1. **She wasn't wearing any**
2. **Her panties showed through**
3. **She stuffed her bra**

Her black panties were visible through the lime-green jumpsuit. *Time 10-18-71*

The 1st feature produced mostly at Walt Disney Feature Animation Florida, Disney's state-of-the-art animation studio, was—you got me! Was it. . . ?
1. *The Little Mermaid*
2. *Hercules*
3. *Mulan*

Mulan. [www.disney.com]

You got me which Disney park is the largest in terms of acreage! Is it. . . ?
1. **Magic Kingdom**
2. **EPCOT**
3. **Animal Kingdom**

At 500 acres, it's Animal Kingdom. Walt Disney World totals 30,500 acres, about twice the size of Manhattan. *St. Petersburg Times 4-6-98 and AP 8-28-98*

Put your money where your mouse is

Walt Disney bought most of the land for Disney World on the quiet for an average of $180 an acre. After the news got out, you got me what land adjacent to D-World went for! Was it. . . ?
1. **$180 per acre, the same**
2. **$1,000 per acre**
3. **$80,000 per acre**

$80,000 per acre. *Some Kind of Paradise by Mark Derr*

This Bud's not for you
Orlando wasn't Walt Disney's 1st choice for Disney World—but you got me where he originally planned to put it! Was it. . . ?
1. **Washington, D.C.**
2. **St. Louis**
3. **Long Island**

St. Louis, but he had a falling out with Augustus Busch, of beer fame, over his alcohol-free park. *Some Kind of Paradise by Mark Derr*

Traveller's advisory
The town of Celebration, the planned Disney community a few miles from Disney World, recorded a town first on August 19, 1998—but you got me what! Was it. . . ?
1. **Their 1st rainy day**
2. **Their 1st home sold**
3. **Their 1st violent crime**

After 2 years, the community of Celebration suffered its 1st armed robbery. *AP 8-12-98*

At Walt Disney World, top speed for the Space Mountain rockets is— you got me! Is it. . . ?
1. **28 mph**
2. **42 mph**
3. **65 mph**

28 mph. *Birnbaum's Walt Disney World 1998*

In 1971, the year Disney World opened, Florida was averaging 22 to 23 million visitors per year. Eighty percent came by car, and the average length of stay was 13 days. But you got me how much the average visitor spent per day here in 1971! Was it. . . ?
1. **$8.50**

2. $18.50
3. $118.50

$18.50. And 96% of visitors hailed from east of the Mississippi. *A Study of the Economic Impact of Disney World by The Tampa Tribune and The Tampa Times (1971)*

On December 29, 1986, you got me what record was set at Disney World! Was it. . . ?
1. The highest temperature recorded
2. Most "mouse ears" sold
3. Most people

Disney World set its single-day attendance record to date. *Some Kind of Paradise by Mark Derr*

Opening its doors 11 years to the day after launching the Magic Kingdom, EPCOT became the only Disney park where you could—you got me what! Was it. . . ?
1. Flea-dip your pet
2. Buy alcoholic beverages
3. Have dental work done

Buy alcohol. *Tampa Tribune 10-1-82*

Places where Goofy isn't: tourists and where else to find them

The road more travelled
Visitors arriving in Florida by car come from one state more than any other—but you got me which one! Is it. . . ?
1. Michigan
2. New York
3. Georgia

Georgia ranks #1: 17.6% of car tourists come from Georgia. The highest percentage of tourists arriving by air come from New York. *Florida Statistical Abstract 1997*

There goes the neighborhood

Most people know that London Bridge can now be found in Lake Havasu City, Arizona—but you got me where Spain's Cloisters of St. Bernard de Clairvaux is! Is it. . . ?
1. **Miami**
2. **St. Augustine**
3. **Pensacola**

Also known as the Spanish Monastery, the 12th-century monastery was bought by publisher William Randolph Hearst for a cool half million. After 29 years in a Brooklyn warehouse, the jigsaw puzzle of the monastery was reassembled in Miami. *St. Petersburg Times 12-5-81*

On Christmas day 1926, John Ringling, one of the 5 famous circus brothers, moved into Cà d'Zan, his historic Sarasota mansion. But you got me what *Cà d'Zan* means! Is it. . . ?
1. **"Thirteen steps"**
2. **"House of John"**
3. **"Three rings"**

In the Venetian dialect, "house of John." *Cà d'Zan brochure*

🎪 BONUS Cà d'Zan question
Architectural elements for John Ringling's Italianate baroque villa, Cà d'Zan, in Sarasota, were drawn from the Doge's Palace in Venice and a tower—but you got me which one! Was it. . . ?
1. **The Leaning Tower of Pisa**
2. **The Tower of London**
3. **The tower of the old Madison Square Garden**

The tower of the old Madison Square Garden. *Historic Homes of Florida by Laura Stewart and Suzanne Hupp*

Descendants of Ernest Hemingway's cats still roam the Key West house, at 907 Whitehead Street, where he wrote 75% of his life's work—but you got me what characteristic distinguishes those cats! Is it. . . ?
1. **They're hairless**
2. **They're six-toed**
3. **They each have 1 blue eye and 1 brown eye**

The cats are six-toed. *Historical Traveler's Guide to Florida by Eliot Kleinberg*

Happy campers in history

You got me what name was given to the early tourists who began arriving here in 1920 in their own cars and camping out! Were they known as. . . ?

1. **Tin-can tourists**
2. **Tin-pan tenters**
3. **Tin Lizzie campers**

Often bringing their own canned foods in their Tin Lizzies, they were Tin-can tourists. *St. Petersburg Times 1-12-98*

Just when you thought it was safe to go to a theme park

In the movie *Jaws 3-D*, a shark terrorizes a Florida theme park—but you got me which one! Is it. . . ?

1. **Sea World**
2. **Marineland**
3. **Adventure Island**

Sea World. The 1983 movie was renamed *Jaws III* for TV and video. *Shot on This Site by William A. Gordon*

When good vermin go bad

The historic palace of Vizcaya, in Miami, boasted a bunch of critters that took to bearing their young in the urns on the patio and nipping the guests. But you got me what kind of creatures! Were they. . . ?

1. **Red foxes**
2. **Raccoons**
3. **Loggerhead turtles**

Raccoons. *St. Petersburg Times 9-4-77*

What are you driving at?

In 1906 the 1st St. Petersburg tourist to arrive by car pulled in after 14 days on the road—but you got me where he came from! Was it. . . ?

1. **New York**
2. **Detroit**
3. **Philadelphia**

Detroit. *St. Petersburg Times 8-1-76*

BONUS early-visitor question

The Florida State Chamber of Commerce figured that during the 1930s tourists came here for an average of 2 weeks and spent an

average of—you got me! Was it. . . ?
1. $112
2. $211
3. $313

$112 for 2 weeks. 1,730,000 tourists visited in 1930; in 1997, 43.5 million, according to the Florida Tourism Marketing Corp. *Tampa Tribune 11-24-40 and St. Petersburg Times 2-18-98*

Silver Springs is supposedly the home of one kind of boat—but you got me what kind! Is it. . . ?
1. Kayak
2. Glass-bottom boat
3. Cigarette boat

A man named John Morrell supposedly stuck a glass pane in the bottom of a rowboat and invented the 1st glass-bottom boat. In 1873 Silver Springs pulled in 50,000 visitors with its glass-bottom boats. *The Springs of Florida by Doug Stamin and St. Petersburg Times 1-12-98*

Labor of love
25 miles south of Miami, Edward Leedskalnin built Coral Castle, by some accounts, for the girl of his dreams back in his native Latvia. But you got me which of the following weighed more! Was it. . . ?
1. The heaviest rocks in the Great Pyramid in Egypt
2. The heaviest coral rocks in Coral Castle
3. Edward Leedskalnin himself

Coral Castle boasts coral rocks weighing up to 35 tons, 3 times heavier than rocks in the Great Pyramid. Leedskalnin was in the under-120-pound range, and he took the secret of how he moved those rocks to the grave with him in 1951. *Tampa Tribune-Times 6-15-77 and Travel (reprint) in Coral Castle brochure*

Good to the last drop
When *Amusement Today* magazine (August 1998) ranked the top steel roller coasters in the world, how many in the top 5 could be found at Busch Gardens, Tampa? Was it. . . ?
1. 1
2. 2
3. All 5

Busch Gardens's roller coasters Montu and Kumba were #3 and #4.

The #1 slot was filled by the Magnum XL-200 at Cedar Point.
[www.buschgardens.com]

Before it became one of the most beautiful public pools, the Venetian
Pool in Coral Gables started out as—you got me! Was it a. . . ?
1. Stone quarry
2. Oil well
3. Sinkhole

Much of the rock used to build Coral Gables came from the quarry
that became the Venetian Pool. *Highlights of Greater Miami 1946 by
J. Calvin Mills*

Where's the reef?
Just north of Key Largo, between mile markers 104 and 105 on the
Overseas Highway, John Pennecamp State Park was the 1st park of its
kind in the country. But you got me what was so unique about it! Is it
that. . . ?
1. It's completely paved
2. It's undersea
3. No humans are allowed

Established in 1960 to protect a 20-mile stretch of the only living
coral reef in the continental U.S., John Pennecamp is the U.S.'s 1st
undersea park. *New York Times 3-13-77 and National Geographic Jan
1962*

High and dry
You got me what tourist attraction can be found on the highest point
(a towering 295 feet above sea level) in peninsular Florida! Is it. . . ?
1. Disney World
2. The Bok Tower
3. Everglades National Park

Edward Bok's 205-foot-tall Singing Tower, near Lake Wales. Bok was
longtime editor of *Ladies Home Journal. Tampa Tribune 2-1-79 and
The Americanization of Edward Bok: An Autobiography by Edward
Bok*

BONUS Bok Tower question
The Bok Singing Tower is constructed largely of a stone that has the
distinction of being the 1st building stone used in America—but you

got me what it is! Is it. . . ?
1. Coquina
2. Adobe
3. Feldspar

The use of coquina, which is limestone composed of shell and coral fragments, dates back to the building of Fort Marion (Castillo de San Marcos), Spanish missions, and the ruins near New Smyrna. *Florida Conservator Oct 1934*

Pipe dream
In the early 1900s, a plumbing contractor named George Turner planted tropical fruit trees in a St. Petersburg sinkhole and began charging people a nickel to stroll through, marking the beginning of—you got me! Was it. . . ?
1. Cypress Gardens
2. Sunken Gardens
3. St. Petersburg Horticultural College

Sunken Gardens, which closed in 1999. *Gainesville Sun 3-21-76*

Alive and kicking
With legs bound in their shiny mermaid tails, the performers at Weeki Wachee swim in the 74° spring water using a stroke they call—you got me! Is it. . . ?
1. The mermaid crawl
2. The shimmy
3. The snake stroke

The mermaid crawl. The 1st mermaid show was probably October 13, 1947. *Tampa Tribune-Times 5-8-83 and St. Petersburg Times 5-9-83*

Opening at Marineland in 1937, the underwater movie studio, Marine Studios, was the brainchild of the grandson of a famous Russian author—but you got me who! Was he. . . ?
1. Dostoyevsky
2. Turgenev
3. Tolstoy

Ilia A. Tolstoy and W. Douglas Burden, of the American Museum of Natural History, originated Marine Studios. In 1955 Clint Eastwood had his first screen role there in the sequel to *The Creature from the*

Black Lagoon, called *Revenge of the Creature.* Originating in 1928 as the world's first oceanarium, Marineland incorporated in 1940 and became Florida's smallest city. *Marine Studios (1941 brochure), News Journal (Daytona Beach) 3-15-98, and Leonard Maltin's Movie and Video Guide.*

Wish you were here

The 1st postcards were issued in Europe in 1869, and 4 years later in the U.S. Picture postcards originated around 1893. Before 1907 you had to write your message on—you got me! Was it. . . ?
   1. Half of the back, just like today
   2. The front
   3. No messages, only addresses

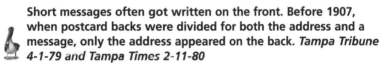

Short messages often got written on the front. Before 1907, when postcard backs were divided for both the address and a message, only the address appeared on the back. *Tampa Tribune 4-1-79 and Tampa Times 2-11-80*

C h a p t e r   1 8

Dropping Names—
Florida Place-Names

Big water

Lake Okeechobee (meaning "big water" in the Seminole language) is the 2nd largest freshwater lake totally in the U.S.—but you got me what's 1st! Is it. . . ?

1. Lake Champlain
2. Lake Michigan
3. Great Salt Lake

Lake Michigan, which is the only 1 of the Great Lakes not shared with Canada. *Guide to the Lake Okeechobee Area by Bill and Carol Gregware*

According to one story, a Brevard County town got its name from an elderly woman who suggested the name she saw on a label—but you got me what town reportedly got its name from a label! Was it. . . ?

1. Cocoa
2. Cracker
3. Chock Full O' Nuts

Cocoa. By some accounts she was standing near a landing at the foot of Willard Street and saw a box of Baker's Cocoa. Another version says the town took Its name from the abundant coco-plums growing in the area. *Florida Place Names by Allen Morris*

Current events

Ponce de León called it "The Cape of Currents," but the name that appeared on the earliest Spanish maps and by which we know it today translates as "a place of roots or cane." But you got me what it is! Is it. . . ?

1. Key Biscayne
2. Dry Tortugas
3. Cape Canaveral

Cape Canaveral. *Florida Place Names by Allen Morris*

What you talkin' 'bout, Willis?

Jai alai means "merry festival" in Basque—but you got me what Vizcaya, the name of the grand Miami estate of James Deering (of International Harvester fame) means in Basque! Is it. . . ?
1. "Elevated place"
2. "House of James"
3. "Mighty wind"

Vizcaya comes from a Basque word meaning "elevated place." Between 1914–1916, about 10% of the population of Miami was involved in its building. *Access: Miami & South Florida and Southern Florida Attractions by Bob Sehlinger and John Finley*

One Hillsborough County town was given its name by the town's 1st postmaster, who combined the names of his 3 daughters—but you got me what town! Was it. . . ?
1. Wimauma
2. Thonotosassa
3. Lake Magdalene

Captain Davis's 3 daughters were *Wi*lma, *Mau*d, and *Ma*ry. *Tampa Times 6-24-62*

Near the General Harney Trail (once Florida's only inland trail from north to south), a town founded on the site of an Indian trading post has an odd name that translates to "happy hunting ground"—but you got me what town! Is it. . . ?
1. Vizcaya
2. Okeechobee
3. Kissimmee

Kissimmee. By other accounts, the name means "Heaven's Place" in the Caloosa Indian language. *Know Florida (State of Florida) and City of Kissimmee/City Information [www.phoenixat.com]*

Spring forward, fall back

On October 9, 1973, a famous Florida spot got its old name back—but you got me what name! Was it. . . ?

1. The Fontainebleau Hotel
2. Cape Canaveral
3. Weeki Wachee

Cape Canaveral was renamed Cape Kennedy by LBJ after the assassination of JFK in November 1963. Cape Canaveral (considered to be the oldest continuously used place-name on the American Atlantic coast) was restored as the geographical point, but the NASA complex remains the John F. Kennedy Space Center. *Tampa Tribune 10-10-73 and U.S. Senate Report No. 92-704*

Eau Gallie was given its name by William Henry Gleason, who was commissioned by the government after the Civil War to survey the territory and determine if it was suitable for "a Negro colony." Eau Gallie means "rocky water"—but you got me in what languages! Are they. . . ?

1. Spanish and French
2. French and Chippewa
3. Swahili and French

Eau is French for water; gallie is a Chippewa Indian word meaning "rocky." *Eau Gallie Chamber of Commerce 1960–1961*

Beam me up, Scotty

A town north of St. Petersburg with strong Scottish ties was, in the 1870s, known informally as Jonesboro and formally as "Florida Township 28 South Range 15 East"—but you got me what it is today! Is it. . . ?

1. Dunedin
2. Tarpon Springs
3. Oldsmar

Dunedin. *St. Petersburg Times 1-20-80*

The small town of Concord, in Gadsden County, was formerly known by a different name that referred to a plague of pests that overran the crops. But you got me what the town was called! Was it. . . ?

1. 'Coon Bottom
2. Locust Corners
3. Skeeterland

In an earlier indefinite time, raccoons apparently overtook the crops in the bottomlands around town, hence the name 'Coon Bottom. *Tampa Tribune 12-20-53*

The town of Ocoee, in Orange County, is often considered the birthplace of the U.S. citrus industry (the 1st commercial citrus nursery was started there by orange budder Capt. B. M. Sims), but its name comes from the Cherokee word for a different fruit—but you got me which one! Is it. . . ?
   1. Grapefruit
   2. Fig
   3. Apricot

The name comes from the Tennessee town, which the Cherokees dubbed *uwagahi,* meaning "apricot vine place." (R. B. F. Roper plotted the area in 1885 and named it for his wife's hometown.) *Florida Place Names by Allen Morris*

The county named Orange County (where Orlando is) by the Territorial Council on Christmas Eve 1824 previously had a buggy name—but you got me what! Was it. . . ?
   1. Mosquito County
   2. Cockroach County
   3. Bee-Sting County

Orange County was 1st known as Mosquito County. *Tampa Sunday Tribune 5-9-54*

That's nice
In Okaloosa County, the Panhandle town of Niceville stands on a spot previously known as—you got me! Is it. . . ?
   1. Stinkytown
   2. Boggy Bayou
   3. Vile-ville

Niceville was the choice of postmaster E. P. Edge, who renamed the place known as Boggy Bayou. *Tampa Times 3-26-62*

Referring to sharp, hidden rocks that gnaw and fray ship cables, the name of one Palm Beach County inlet and town means "mouse's mouth" in Spanish—but you got me what town! Is it. . . ?

1. **Boca Raton**
2. **Punta Gorda**
3. **Wauchula**

 Boca Raton. The name comes from the Spanish nautical term *boca de ratones. Encyclopedia Britannica*

The original Garden of Eden, Liberty County, 1953

Chapter 19

Forty Shades of Green—Florida Greenery

The green stuff: plants and trees

Kind of hip, kind of now, Charlie!
The rare Florida torreya tree gets its nickname from the aroma it gives off, especially when bruised. But you got me what that nickname is! Is it. . . ?
1. The P.U. pine
2. The stinking cedar
3. The what-died willow

Stinking cedar. *Florida Department of Agriculture and Consumer Services*

Great oaks from little acorns
American Forests's *National Register of Big Trees*, 1998–1999, lists the 825 trees that are the biggest of their species. Among the states having the greatest number of champion trees, Florida ranks—you got me! Is it. . . ?
1. Florida has more champion trees than any other state
2. Only California has more champs than Florida
3. Only California and Oregon have more

Florida has more champion trees than any other state. Seven champion trees were blown down by Hurricane Andrew in 1992.
American Forests news release [http://leaf.amfor.org] and Florida Handbook 1997–1998

You got me how long a sapling cypress tree needs to grow a trunk 2 feet in diameter! Is it. . . ?

1. 25 years
2. 50 years
3. 100 years

About 100 years. Cypress is 1 of only 2 timbers native to Florida; the other is pine. *St. Petersburg Times 10-8-78*

Legend has it that in 1823, the Capitol Commission met with an Indian chief under the historic May Oak to discuss the location of Florida's capitol. But you got me who that chief was! Was he. . . ?
1. Chief Tallahassee
2. Chief Pensacola
3. Chief Daytona

Chief Tallahassee. *All-Florida Magazine 4-28-57*

Hatchet job
When you chop down a cypress and drop it in the river, you got me what it's likely to do! Does it. . . ?
1. Float downstream
2. Sink like a stone
3. Turn to mush and disintegrate

It often sinks and never rises. A part of the St. Johns River is said to have a floor of sunken cypresses, reportedly worth millions. *St. Petersburg Times 10-8-78*

In 1884 a Florida woman returned from the Cotton States Exposition in New Orleans with something for her Palatka-area fish pond, but it escaped into the St. Johns River. Today it has overrun most of the waterways in the South and costs taxpayers millions of dollars to control. But you got me what it is! Is it. . . ?
1. Waterhyacinth
2. Walking catfish
3. Brain coral

Waterhyacinth, which every growing season generates 65,000 offspring per plant. Other versions of how the waterhyacinth got here exist. *Environmental Information Center of the Florida Conservation Foundation 1972 and St. Petersburg Times 1-24-77*

Orange you kinda glad we did: oranges and other fruits

How do you like them apples?
According to travel writer John McPhee, most Bolivians won't go near OJ at breakfast; however, they drink it steadily the rest of the day. But you got me what percent of North Americans have OJ with breakfast! Is it. . . ?
1. 5%
2. 20%
3. 52%

20%. Oranges by John McPhee and St. Petersburg Times 8-26-98

Lue Gim Gong, a plant breeder considered the Luther Burbank of Florida, settled in Deland in 1886 and 6 years later developed the Gim Gong Grapefruit—but you got me what was so special about that! Was it that. . . ?
1. It was 10% bigger
2. It was 10 times sweeter
3. It could withstand 10° colder temps

The Gim Gong Grapefruit could take the colder temperatures. *Who Was Who in Florida by Henry S. Marks*

Big whoop
The trio of C. D. Atkins, Louis MacDowell, and Edwin Moore spent 3 years in a government building in Winter Haven developing frozen concentrated OJ for wartime use. But you got me what the trio received for their discovery! Did they get. . . ?
1. Royalties in excess of $7 million annually
2. A Nobel prize
3. Time off

The Agriculture Department grabbed the 1948 patent and the men never saw a dime in royalties, but the three were given 6 months of vacation time. *The Ledger Online (Lakeland) [www.theledger.com]*

Miss America's behaving badly
For 12 years, a former Miss America reigned as the Florida orange juice spokeswoman until she became embroiled in an anti–gay rights campaign in Dade County—but you got me who that was! Was she. . . ?

1. Phyllis George
2. Bess Myerson
3. Anita Bryant

The official line was that Anita Bryant's notoreity and the termination of her contract were unrelated. A similar fate befell Burt Reynolds, whose OJ spokesman contract was not renewed after his bitter divorce from Loni Anderson. *Tampa Tribune 8-31-80 and AP 8-26-98*

Orange crush
In 1954 the 1st cartons of OJ on the market came from—you got me! Was it. . . ?
  1. Sunkist
  2. Dole
  3. Tropicana

Tropicana. *St. Petersburg Times 12-7-81*

BONUS OJ question
More than half of the orange juice imported into the U.S. comes ashore in the city of—you got me! Is it. . . ?
  1. Tampa
  2. Jacksonville
  3. Miami

Tampa; 9 million gallons from Brazil. *American Shipper Jan 1998*

Florida considers herself the birthplace of all but 1 named variety of grapefruit—but you got me which one came from elsewhere! Is it. . . ?
  1. The Texas Ruby Red
  2. The California Pink
  3. The Hawaii Lihue Scarlet

The Texas Ruby Red. *Some Kind of Paradise by Mark Derr*

Do I dare to eat a peach?
You got me how much New Yorkers might have to fork out for a box of premium peaches from Columbia County in the 1870s! Was it. . . ?
  1. 8¢
  2. $8
  3. $80

$8 for a box of peaches, although Sea Island cotton was the chief money crop. *Tampa Sunday Tribune 3-7-54*

The Florida Citrus Commission, watchdog of the state's citrus industry, held their 1st meeting September 10, 1935—but you got me what their #1 problem was at that meeting! Was it. . . ?
1. Tangelos
2. California oranges
3. Adding color to oranges

Color-adding was considered #1 in importance. *Tampa Tribune 3-31-85*

🍊 BONUS citrus-biz question

The Florida Citrus Exchange announced in 1953 that it would begin to advertise its famous Florigold Indian River brand oranges in New York for the 1st time in this way—but you got me how! Was it. . . ?
1. With the Florida orange blimp
2. On the back cover of the fledgling *TV Guide*
3. On television

It began advertising on the morning program *The Josephine McCarthy Show*, on WNBC-TV. On NY radio, it bought time on WOR's *McCann's At Home* and WEVD's *News of the Day*. Seald-Sweet *Scratch Pad (Florida Citrus Exchange, Oct 1953)*

Columbus brought citrus to the New World (Haiti, actually) on his 2nd trip in 1493—but the first citrus trees brought into Florida actually came from—you got me! Was it. . . ?
1. Spain
2. China
3. Cuba

Cuban fishermen brought them around 1815 and planted them from Charlotte Harbor to the Anclote River. *Tampa Port Magazine Dec 1962*

Picking a peck

You got me what percentage of Florida oranges are harvested by hand! Is it. . . ?
1. 4%
2. 53%
3. 98%

98%. *The Story of Florida Orange Juice by Chet Townsend*

[http://members.aol.com/citrusweb/oj_story.html]

Mutants among us

A mutant fruit was introduced to these parts in 1823 by French physician Count Odet Philippe. It's called a *toronja* in Spanish and *pomelo*
in Portuguese—but you got me what we call it! Is it. . . ?

1. Watermelon
2. Grapefruit
3. Tomato

Grapefruit, so called because they grow in clusters like grapes. *Some
Kind of Paradise by Mark Derr*

BONUS grapefruit question

In the 1982 bumper crop of grapefruit, you got me how many grapefruit Florida grew for every man, woman, and child in the nation!
Was it. . . ?

1. 5
2. 10
3. 20

Twenty. *Tampa Tribune 6-20-82*

You got me how much of the world's crop of oranges, tangerines, and
grapefruit came from Florida in the year 1930! Was it. . . ?

1. Only about 5%
2. About a third
3. All of it

**About 33%. Today, about 70% of the nation's orange crop comes
from Florida, with most of the remainder coming from California.**
*Tampa Morning Tribune 5-7-54 and World Book Multimedia
Encyclopedia*

You got me how long it takes, on average, for Florida citrus to ripen
after it's picked! Is it. . . ?

1. 2 days
2. About 1 week
3. It doesn't

Citrus has to ripen *on* the tree, not after it's picked. *The Story of*

Florida Orange Juice by Chet Townsend [http://members.aol.com/ citrusweb/oj_story.html]

🏝 BONUS orange question

You got me what you call the fruit that's a cross between an orange, a tangerine, and a grapefruit! Is it. . . ?

1. **Ugli**
2. **Barfi**
3. **Yucki**

 "Ugli" is the trademark name for the fruit that has a yellowish, wrinkled rind. *American Heritage Dictionary*

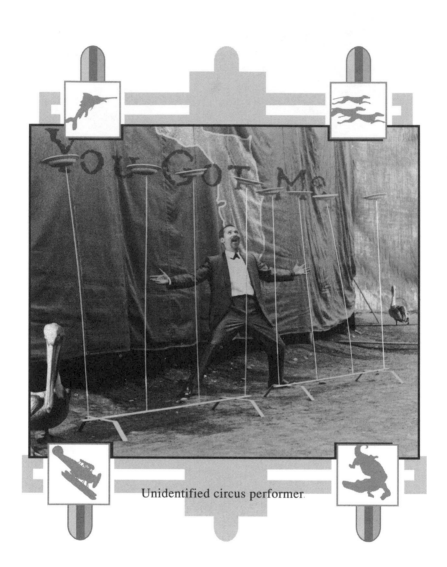

Unidentified circus performer.

Chapter 20

It Figures—Florida in Numbers

Sticks and stones may break my bones

According to risk statistics, Americans in 1996 suffered a greater number of injuries from—you got me! Is it. . . ?
1. Shark attacks
2. Buckets
3. Toilets

There were 43,687 injuries associated with toilets (that's not including toilet-bowl products); 10,907 from buckets and pails; but only 18 injuries and deaths from sharks. *[www.flmnh.ufl.edu]*

A lot of living to do

In terms of life expectancy, you got me how Florida ranks nationwide! Is it. . . ?

1. Florida has the longest life expectancy
2. Only Hawaii has a longer one
3. Only Hawaii, California, and Arizona have longer one

Life expectancy is longest in Florida. *Florida Handbook 1997–1998*

Pressing the flesh

According to 1998 statistics from the Florida Department of State, 17,702 people on the state's voter rolls were found to be—you got me! Were they. . . ?
1. Foreign nationals
2. Dead
3. Underage

There were 17,702 dead people on the rolls, and over 50 thousand felons. *St. Petersburg Times 8-19-98*

In 1990 the median age of all Florida year-round residents was—you got me! Was it. . . ?
1. A touch over 36
2. A touch over 46
3. A touch over 56

A touch over 36. *The Florida Survival Handbook by Mike Vizcary*

Get a move on
According to 1990 IRS stats, 55,679 more New Yorkers moved to Florida than vice-versa. But you got me how North Carolina stacked up! Did. . . ?
1. More Tarheels move to Florida
2. More Floridians move to NC
3. It was a dead heat—1 came for every 1 that left

19,391 Floridians moved to NC, but only 15,769 Tarheels moved to Florida. *Florida Handbook 1997–1998*

BONUS moving question
According to a 1997 study of housing turnover rates, the average Florida home gets a new owner every—you got me how many years! Is it. . . ?
1. 6.2 years—the fastest turnover rate in the U.S.
2. 12.7 years—about the U.S. average for the last 26 years
3. 18.3 years—the nation's slowest

At 12.7 years, Florida was at about the national average since 1972 (12.5). Arizona was 6.2; New York was 18.3. *Chicago Title and Trust Co. [www.westerndivision.ctt.com]*

You got me how much it would cost in 1876 to telegraph 10 words from Havana to New York using the Florida lines of the International Ocean Telegraph Company! Was it. . . ?
1. $1
2. $2
3. $5

Tariff between NY and Havana was $5 for 10 words. *Telegraph in America by James D. Reid*

Take-home pay
Around 1927, an 8- to 10-room "luxury" home in Tampa's most fashionable neighborhoods was renting for—you got me! Was it. . . ?
1. $50/month
2. $150/month
3. $550/month

$150/month unfurnished. The same house in "less pretentious but . . . presentable" neighborhoods, $100; small houses, $25 to $35. *Tampa Truisms: Annual Statistical Edition Jan 1927*

On ice
You got me what a pound of ice, "in season," shipped to inland Florida would run you in 1845! Was it. . . ?
1. 10¢
2. $1
3. $10

$1 per pound. Liquor to pour over that ice went for about 30¢ a gallon. *Florida State Chamber of Commerce 1945*

According to statistics from 1938, one Florida city could boast 196 people worth in excess of $100,000—but you got me which city! Was it. . . ?
1. Jacksonville
2. Miami
3. Tampa

Tampa. Jacksonville had 180 people worth 100 grand, Miami only 103, and St. Petersburg, 72. More than half of all Floridians worth over 5 grand lived in those cities. *Tampa Chamber of Commerce 1938*

Today, Florida ranks 4th in population nationwide, up from 13th in 1957. But you got me where we ranked at the turn of the 20th century! Was it. . . ?
1. 22nd
2. 33rd
3. 44th

33rd. Not until the 1930 census did Florida pass the 1 million mark. *Tampa Times 7-24-57 and Florida Library Survey 1935*

Stuck in Margaritaville

In an historical account of Key West before the fire of March 30, 1886, a reporter for the *New York Sun* put the population at about 15,000 (there were over 100 cigar factories there at the time) and said that if a person wasn't too particular, he could live a week in Key West for— you got me! Was it. . . ?

1. 75¢
2. $7.50
3. $75

75¢ is what the reporter said: pineapples cost 1¢, bananas 10¢ a bunch, hominy is cheap, and a string of fish can be caught. *Key West, Fla. Before the Fire of March 30th, 1886 by "The New York Sun Man"*

I got your number

In c.1906 Jacksonville, you got me which number was the greatest! Was it. . . ?

1. The number of sewer workers
2. The miles of paved streets
3. The number of arrests

 Arrests numbered 3,811; 37 of the city's 135 miles of streets were paved; the sewer department employed 12 men. Other useless numbers: 51 firemen, 77 cops, 12,000 books in the library. *Mercantile and Industrial Review of Jacksonville, Florida, by the Industrial Department of the Seaboard Air Line Railway*

Chapter 21

To the Moon, Alice—
Florida in Space

Technically speaking
In December 1958 a giant Atlas satellite from Cape Canaveral transmitted the first voice communication from space back to Earth—but you got me what it beamed down! Was it. . . ?
1. "Hello Mudda, Hello Fadduh"
2. "That's one small step for a man, one giant leap for mankind."
3. President Eisenhower's Christmas message

President Eisenhower's Christmas message. *UPI 12-20-58*

Able and Baker, the 1st animals to survive a U.S. space flight, were launched May 28, 1959, from Cape Canaveral. But you got me what kind of creatures they were! Were they. . . ?
1. Mice
2. Monkeys
3. Collies

Able was a rhesus monkey, and Baker, a spider monkey. *Facts on File 5-28 to 6-3-59*

At 11:38 A.M. on January 28, 1986, the space shuttle carrying 7 astronauts, including the 1st private citizen to fly on the space shuttle (NH social studies teacher, Sharon Christa McAuliffe), exploded 73 seconds after liftoff from Cape Canaveral. The shuttle was the. . . ?
1. *Columbia*
2. *Stars and Stripes*
3. *Challenger*

The space shuttle *Challenger. Tampa Tribune 1-29-86 and The People's Chronology*

First launch of the Space Shuttle, Cape Canaveral, April 12,1981

The case for triskaidekaphobia

You got me what flight launched at unlucky 1313 hours (1:13) CST and was headed for the moon on April 13 when an oxygen tank exploded and they had to limp home. Was it. . . ?

1. *Apollo 13*
2. *Gemini 13*
3. *Mercury 13*

Apollo 13, carrying astronauts Lovell, Haise, and Swigert. (Triskaidekaphobia is fear of the number 13.) *St. Petersburg Times 11-20-81*

Racking up the frequent-flier miles

On February 20, 1962, John Glenn lifted off from Launch Complex 14 at Cape Kennedy in his *Friendship 7* capsule and became the 1st American to orbit Earth. But you got me how many sunrises Glenn saw in that one day! Was it. . . ?

1. 1
2. 2
3. 3

Glenn saw his 3rd sunrise of the day over the Pacific at 12:28 PM (EST); he went around 3 times during a journey of 4 hours, 55 minutes. Glenn returned to space 10-29-98. *UPI 2-21-62 and AP 2-21-72 and St. Petersburg Times 10-29-98*

The 1st missile was launched from Cape Canaveral, on July 24, in—you got me what year! Was it. . . ?

1. 1950
2. 1955
3. 1960

A 2-stage Bumper missile that used a German V-2 and an Army WAC-Corporal took off July 24, 1950. The Army Redstone, the U.S.'s 1st ballistic missile, debuted in 1953. *Tampa Tribune 12-6-59*

Bring in da noise

You got me which is loudest! Is it a. . . ?

1. Space shuttle launch
2. Jet takeoff
3. Circular saw

The space shuttle cranks up to about 170 decibels; a jet goes 140–160, a saw 100–110, and a whisper about 20–30. *St. Petersburg Times 6-30-98*

BONUS space shuttle question
You got me how fast the space shuttle is going as it clears the tower! Is it. . . ?
1. Only about 30 mph
2. Around 100 mph
3. Mach 1

The shuttle is reaching 100 mph as it clears the tower. *Aviation History [www.historynet.com]*

Space race
During the 1st missile launch at Cape Canaveral at the beginning of the space age, a Jeep raced back and forth on the sandy road to the launch pad in order to frighten off—you got me! Was it. . . ?
1. Spies
2. Tourists
3. Snakes

Poisonous snakes. *Tampa Tribune 12-6-59*

Shoot the moon
You got me when the U.S. made its 1st attempt to shoot a rocket to the moon! Was it August 17. . . ?
1. 1958
2. 1964
3. 1967

In 1958 a Thor-Able rocket for the moon exploded shortly after take-off. *Tampa Tribune 12-6-59*

Space, the final frontier
The original name for Project Mercury, the 1st U.S. manned space program, was—you got me! Was it. . . ?
1. Project Kennedy
2. Man in Space Soonest
3. Human Cannonball Program

Man in Space Soonest. *Aviation History [www.historynet.com]*

Nobody can hear you scream

California astrophysicist Sally Ride finally broke through the glass ceiling in the American space program. But you got me how many years the U.S. space program had been manned by men only! Was it. . . ?

1. 12 years
2. 17 years
3. 22 years

Ride rode the *Challenger* in 1983, 22 years after the nation's 1st manned space flight. *St. Petersburg Times 6-19-83*

One of the largest buildings in the world, the Vehicle Assembly Building at Kennedy Space Center is like a garage for the space shuttles. But you got me which is higher! Is it. . . ?

1. The high bay doors of the VAB
2. The Statue of Liberty
3. The Eiffel Tower

The VAB doors are 456 feet high, higher than the 305-foot Statue of Liberty. The Eiffel Tower, however, stands 984 feet. *[www.ksc.nasa.gov] and Encyclopedia Britannica*

Chapter 22

This is Your Brain in Florida—Florida Education

In 1995 the University of Florida raked in $4,516,485 in royalties from the 1965 invention of—you got me! Is it. . . ?
1. **Frisbees**
2. **Gatorade**
3. **Cap'n Crunch**

Gatorade (now a division of the Quaker Oats company) was invented at UF. *"UF aided by lucrative patents" by Sarah Eisenhauer [www. alligator.org] and [www.gatorade.com]*

If you've got to ask how much it costs
When Rollins College in Winter Park opened its doors November 4, 1885, the total expenses for the year, including tuition, room with a furnished light, and board, amounted to—you got me! Was it. . . ?
1. **$34**
2. **$234**
3. **$634**

Tuition was $18 for each of 3 terms, board was $48 (later $36), and the room was $12, for a total of $234 per year. In 1999 a year for a full-time undergrad in a double room runs in excess of $27 thousand. *Rollins College Bulletin Dec 1955 and Rollins College Admissions Office*

BONUS Rollins question
In 1992 Rollins College communications student Leanza Cornett was thrust into the national spotlight when she—you got me! Did she. . . ?
1. **Wed Sylvester Stallone**
2. **Win Miss America**
3. **Swam from Cuba to Key West**

Cornett was the 1st Miss Florida to win the Miss America pageant. *Facts on File 9-24-92 and St. Petersburg Times 9-10-80*

When the University of Florida came into existence in 1905 with an enrollment of only 100, it was one of the few state universities in the nation which were not—you got me! Was it not. . . ?
1. Accredited
2. Coed
3. Free

Coed. The University of Florida at Gainesville was established for men, Florida State College at Tallahassee for women. *Tampa Tribune 1-1-33*

Florida A&M University awarded its 1st honorary doctorate in 1983 to Guy Bluford Jr.—but you got me who Bluford is! Is he. . . ?
1. The 1st African-American to fly in space
2. The man who discovered the Titanic's watery grave
3. Florida A&M's 1st and only Heisman Trophy winner

Bluford flew aboard the *Challenger* in 1983 and was America's 1st black astronaut. *Tampa Tribune 10-15-83*

Toga! Toga! Toga!
At UF's predecessor, the East Florida Seminary, at the turn of the century coeds had to wear uniforms that included blue serge skirts and shirtwaists in winter (duck in summer), topped off with a black or dark blue—you got me! Was it a. . . ?
1. Sailor hat
2. Rain bonnet
3. Panama hat

Sailor hats. *Tampa Tribune 6-14-59*

No dark sarcasm in the classroom
Dade County's 1st school opened March 1886 with pupils aged 6–17. The teacher was Miss Hattie Gale—but you got me how old Hattie was! Was she. . . ?
1. 15
2. 75
3. 85

Fifteen. *Tampa Tribune 1-26-58*

The Wright stuff

The largest single-site grouping of buildings by famed architect Frank Lloyd Wright are the 12 built between 1938 and 1958 on the campus of—you got me! Are they at. . . ?

1. Central Florida
2. Florida Southern
3. Florida A&M

Florida Southern College in Lakeland. *Frank Lloyd Wright: A Biography of Material in Roux Library, Florida Southern College by Randall M. MacDonald*

With only $1.50 to her name and 5 students, this daughter of former slaves founded in 1904 the Daytona Educational and Industrial Training School for Negro Girls—but you got me who this famous educator was! Was she. . . ?

1. Mary McLeod Bethune
2. Rosemary Barkett
3. May Mann Jennings

Mary McLeod Bethune's school merged with Cookman Institute in 1923 to form Bethune-Cookman College. *The Ledger Online (Lakeland) [www.theledger.com]*

Now is the time for all good men to come to the aid of the party

Playboy magazine only 1 time ranked the 40 best "party" schools in the nation, in their January 1987 issue. California State University at Chico topped the list—but you got me which Florida school came in 2nd! Was it. . . ?

1. Florida State
2. University of Florida
3. University of Miami

Miami came in 2nd. The only other Florida school to make the list was the University of Florida (#29). On the Princeton Review's 1998 list of the top 10 "party schools," UF was #3 and FSU was #6. *[www.playboy.com] and AP 8-24-98*

On December 6, 1978, Florida Technological University outside Orlando underwent a name change—but you got me what it became! Today is it. . . ?

1. University of North Florida
2. University of Central Florida
3. University of South Florida

Originally opened in 1963, FTU became the University of Central Florida. [www.orgs.ucf.edu]

Gov. Thomas Broome, in 1853, signed a bill creating Florida's 1st state-supported institution of higher learning, which was—you got me! Was it. . . ?
1. Florida State
2. Broome Community College
3. East Florida Seminary

The East Florida Seminary in Ocala, which evolved into the University of Florida. Around 1900 tuition was $10, and a year of school ran about $185 at UF. *Tampa Tribune 2-9-54 and 6-14-59*

The names Cosmopolitan University of Florida, Orange Blossom State University, Ponce de León University, and the University of Florida's South West Coast University were some of the proposed names for the Tampa university that admitted its 1st class in 1960—but you got me what name they finally settled on! Was it. . . ?
1. Sun Coast University
2. Florida Southwestern
3. University of South Florida

Ground was broken for the University of South Florida in September 1958. *Tampa Times 7-16-57 and 9-4-58*

🏃 BONUS USF question

While a USF student, this performer, whose act features the watermel-on-smashing "Sledge-o-matic," led a cafeteria protest by driving a trailer full of pigs onto campus. But you got me who that was! Was that. . . ?
1. Gallagher
2. Elayne Boosler
3. Hulk Hogan

Gallagher, whose 1st name is Leo. Elayne Boosler and Hulk Hogan were also USF students. *Tampa Tribune 9-25-94 and [www. usfbulls.com]*

Spook central

By 1962 the largest CIA station in the world (outside Langley), and the only full-service operation ever on U.S. soil, was located on the campus of—you got me! Was it. . . ?

    1. **University of Miami**
    2. **Eckerd College**
    3. **Palm Beach Community College**

The University of Miami's south campus was home to the CIA's JM/WAVE operation against Castro's Cuba. *Miami by Joan Didion and Shadow Warrior by Felix Rodriguez and John Weisman*

🪝BONUS UM question

The mascot of the University of Miami Hurricanes is—you got me! Is it. . . ?

    1. **Stormy**
    2. **The Ibis**
    3. **Gator**

The Ibis. *Hurricanes Handbook by Jim Martz*

The land on which Henry B. Plant built his grand Tampa Bay Hotel (today Plant Hall at the University of Tampa) was picked up from one Jesse Hayden, who himself had come into the land by trading something for it—but you got me what! Did he trade a. . . ?

    1. **Hair-growing tonic**
    2. **Grapefruit orchard**
    3. **Horse and wagon**

Hayden got the 60 acres in exchange for a white horse and a wagon. *The University of Tampa Foundation 1966*

In 1971, when a drug-store magnate donated $10 million to the floundering Florida Presbyterian College in St. Petersburg, they showed their appreciation by naming the college after him. But you got me what college that is! Is it. . . ?

    1. **Stetson University**
    2. **Eckerd College**
    3. **Rollins College**

Florida Presbyterian (founded 1958) officially became Eckerd College on July 1, 1972. *Tampa Tribune 4-19-64 and Tampa Tribune-Times 11-7-71*

In 1905 the newly established Florida State College for Women had 204 students and a campus that consisted of—you got me how many buildings! Was it. . . ?
1. 1
2. 4
3. 9

2 dorms, a gym, and 1 academic building. *The Florida Tourist Guide Oct 1929*

Where the world comes for sun and fire safety violations
Although the numbers of students flocking to Florida were bolstered by the film *Where The Boys Are*, the 1st spring-break boom started in the 1930s when one city invited college students down to the first "Annual College Swim Forum." But you got me what city that was! Was it. . . ?
1. Cocoa Beach
2. Daytona Beach
3. Fort Lauderdale

 Fort Lauderdale received its record number of spring breakers in 1985, a number estimated at 350,000. Nearly 550,000 flocked to places like Panama City Beach in 1998. *Tampa Tribune 3-26-61, Tampa Tribune-Times 4-15-73, Fodor's '93 Florida, and Life 3-99*

Chapter 23

On with the Show, This is It—Florida Media

Radio days

Talking heads

In 1945 Gainesville native Martha Rountree debuted a radio show that went over to NBC television two years later and was moderated by Lawrence Spivack until 1975—but you got me what show that was! Was it. . . ?

1. *What's My Line*
2. *Meet The Press*
3. *Winky Dink*

The panel show *Meet The Press*. *Current Biography 1957 and People's Chronology*

Hair raising

One Jacksonville native and radio personality gained fame as "queen of the hillbillies" and was responsible for the pigtail fad that swept college campuses in 1943—but you got me who she was! Was she. . . ?

1. Maybelle Carter
2. Judy Canova
3. Minnie Pearl

Judy Canova. Her daughter Diana Canova starred in the TV sitcom *Soap*. *St. Petersburg Times 7-17-83*

All talk

One broadcaster and CNN personality started his long radio career at WAHR in Miami, where on May 1, 1957, moments before going on the air, he changed his last name from Zeiger to—you got me! Is it. . . ?

"Indian" aerialist, 1950s postcard

1. King
2. Limbaugh
3. Osgood

Lawrence Harvey Zeiger became Larry King. *Current Biography Yearbook 1985*

In 1922 the U.S. Department of Commerce licensed WDAE as Florida's 1st broadcast radio station—but you got me where WDAE was! Was it in. . . ?
1. Jacksonville
2. Tampa
3. Miami

Tampa. WDAE, which promoted itself as "Wonderful Days and Evenings" (to employees: "We Don't Always Eat"), began regularly scheduled programming 5-31-22. It broadcast the nation's 1st complete church service and possibly the nation's 1st singing commercial (a Ford dealership). *Tampa Tribune 9-25-94*

Catchin' a little tube

Known as "Mr. Saturday Night" during TV's Golden Age, this portly entertainer relocated his CBS variety show to Miami Beach so that he could play golf year-round—but you got me who he was! Was he. . . ?
1. Sid Caesar
2. Milton Berle
3. Jackie Gleason

Jackie Gleason died in Fort Lauderdale on June 24, 1987. *Annual Obituary 1987 and [www.bibliomag.com]*

On April 3, 1953, the son of an émigré to Miami appeared on the very 1st cover of *TV Guide*—but you got me whose son that was! Was it. . . ?
1. Desi Arnaz's son
2. Zsa Zsa Gabor's
3. Harry Belafonte's

Weighing 8 lbs, 9 oz, Desiderio Alberto Arnaz IV appeared on the cover of the inaugural *TV Guide*. *TV Guide Classic Cover Gallery [www.tvgen.com]*

Tweezed, perky, and talented too?

Orlando's Delta Burke (*Designing Women*) won the Miss Florida title in 1974 and went on to the Miss America pageant, where she won the talent contest. But you got me what Delta's talent was! Did she. . . ?

1. Baton twirl
2. Play the oboe
3. Recite an original soliloquy

She recited an original soliloquy of Anne Boleyn awaiting beheading.
St. Petersburg Times 1-2-83

Sign off

In 1997 somebody ripped off the street sign on State Road A1A in Brevard County for I DREAM OF JEANNIE LANE. But you got me what Florida town was the home of Jeannie and Capt. Tony Nelson! Was it. . . ?

1. Titusville
2. Jupiter
3. Cocoa Beach

Cocoa Beach. The Barbara Eden–Larry Hagman sitcom ran from September 1965 to September 1970. *Florida Today 2-21-97 [www. flatoday.com] and Television Comedy Series by Joel Eisner and David Krinsky*

Don't go there

CBS's *60 Minutes* did a 1974 story on Hillsborough County. Its message to Northerners considering a move to the Tampa Bay area was—you got me! Was it. . . ?

1. Come on in, the water's fine
2. Look before you leap
3. If it's good enough for Andy Rooney . . .

Look before you leap, in response to the county's explosive growth.
Tampa Tribune 2-11-74

You got me who Miami retirees Dorothy Zbornak, Rose Nyland, Blanche Devereaux, and Sophia Petrillo are! Are they. . . ?

1. The Golden Girls
2. The owners of Gentle Ben
3. Organists at Pro Player Stadium

The Golden Girls ran from 1985 to 1992. *[www.innotts.co.uk]*

From 1974 until 1988, NBC television coverage of the Orange Bowl parade was hosted by—you got me! Was it. . . ?

1. **Joe Garagiola**
2. **Willard Scott**
3. **Joe Namath**

Joe Garagiola served as parade host 14 times. *[http://cbs.sportsline.com]*

In 1996 the 5th season of this MTV series featured cast members Dan, Sarah, Flora, Melissa, Mike, Joe, Cynthia, and Leroy the dog, who lived together in a house on Rivo Alto in Miami. But you got me what show that was! Was it. . . ?

1. *The Real World*
2. *Celebrity Deathmatch*
3. *Road Rules*

The Real World. **Melissa, the only Florida native, is a UM graduate.** *The Real World by James Soloman and [www.mtv.com]*

Image is everything: on-screen Florida

Miami native Sidney Poitier became the 1st African-American to win the Best Actor Academy Award when he took home the Oscar for 1963's—you got me! Was it. . . ?

1. *To Sir With Love*
2. *Lilies of the Field*
3. *In the Heat of the Night*

Lilies of the Field. Interesting People/Black American History Makers by George L. Lee

Filmed on locations in Seaside and Panama City, this 1998 movie starred Jim Carrey as an insurance salesman who is unaware that his entire life is on the air. But you got me what movie that is! Is it. . . ?

1. *Liar, Liar*
2. *Ace Ventura*
3. *The Truman Show*

The Truman Show, **directed by Peter Weir.** *Ace Ventura* **was shot in Miami.** *Internet Movie Database [us.imdb.com]*

In 1993 a Hollywood celeb bought an extravagant Biscayne Bay–front estate in the Cliff Hammocks neighborhood, for which he coughed up $8 million—then a Dade County record for a private home! But you got me who! Was it. . . ?

1. **Sylvester Stallone**
2. **Arnold Schwarzenegger**
3. **Burt Reynolds**

Sylvester Stallone. At this writing, the 5-bedroom estate is on the market for the asking price of $27.5 million. *Miami Herald [www.goflorida.com] and St. Petersburg Times 10-2-98*

Men in tights

The movie *The Turning Point* featured the ballet star who founded (with choreographer Mark Morris) the White Oak Dance Project, based in Yulee, on the White Oak Plantation. But you got me who that dancer is! Is he. . . ?

1. **Mikhail Baryshnikov**
2. **Aleksandr Kirov**
3. **Rudolf Nureyev**

Baryshnikov, who defected from the Soviet Union in 1974. *[www.suite101.com] and Encyclopedia Britannica*

Not off to see the wizard

One-time University of Florida premed student Buddy Ebsen (Jed Clampett on *The Beverly Hillbillies*) originally landed a plum role in the 1939 classic *The Wizard of Oz*, only to land himself in the hospital. But you got me what part! Was he going to be. . . ?

1. **The Wizard**
2. **Uncle Henry**
3. **The Tin Man**

Buddy Ebsen was cast as the Tin Man, but the pure-aluminum silver powder got in his lungs and made him deathly ill. Jack Haley replaced him. *People Online and [www.mindspring.com]*

In Jacksonville in 1914, the corpulent half of a famous comedy duo got his big break in movies when he was paid $15 for 3 days' work making the film *Outwitting Dad*—but you got me who he was! Was he. . . ?

1. Oliver Hardy
2. Lou Costello
3. Fatty Arbuckle

Georgian Oliver Hardy was working as a cabaret singer billed as "The Ton of Jollity" at the time. By 1916 Jacksonville had 30 film companies. *Dreamers, Schemers and Scalawags by Stuart B. McIver*

Eighteen miles north of Tampa, outside Wesley Chapel, 44 homes in the Carpenter's Run development had their homes repainted in pastel shades for a movie about a man-made boy played by Johnny Depp. But you got me what movie that was! Was it. . . ?
1. *Edward Scissorhands*
2. *The Nightmare Before Christmas*
3. *The Elephant Man*

Edward Scissorhands **(1990), directed by Tim Burton.** *Shot on This Site by William A. Gordon*

This Bascom, Florida, native, who cut her acting teeth at the University of Florida, earned 2 Academy Award nominations for *Bonnie & Clyde* and *Chinatown* before taking home the Oscar for *Network*. But you got me who she is! Is she. . . ?
1. Sally Field
2. Faye Dunaway
3. Sally Kellerman

Faye Dunaway, born January 14, 1941, in Bascom. *Encyclopedia of Southern Culture*

Name change
In 1952 the town of Rock Harbor changed its name to the name of a movie that was (partly) filmed there—but you got me what name it took! Was it. . . ?
1. Peyton Place
2. Key Largo
3. Cape Fear

The town on the island of Key Largo was called Rock Harbor until its P.O.'s name was changed to Key Largo after the Bogart–Bacall movie, their last together. *Florida Place Names by Allen Morris*

You got me in which movie a character named Ratso Rizzo says, "Miami Beach. That's where you could score. Anybody could score there. . . ." Was it. . . ?
1. *Midnight Cowboy*
2. *Moon Over Miami*
3. *In the Good Old Summertime*

Dustin Hoffman played Ratso Rizzo in *Midnight Cowboy*. The bus at the end of the movie pulls into Coral Gables. *The Movie Quote Book by Harry Haun and Hollywood East by Ames Ponti*

The highest-grossing film in Florida's history was shot in Miami and Fort Lauderdale in only 6 days. But you got me what movie that was! Was it. . . ?
1. *Star Wars*
2. *Creature from the Black Lagoon*
3. *Deep Throat*

Deep Throat* was made for $24 thousand and has earned over $300 million. *Hollywood East by Ames Ponti

All singing, all dancing
Although best known for the role of the Leading Player in the musical *Pippin*, this Floridian had his 1st leading Broadway role in *Jesus Christ Superstar*. But you got me who he is! Is he. . . ?
1. Michael Crawford
2. Ben Vereen
3. Bob Fosse

Ben Vereen was born 10-10-46 in Miami, raised in Brooklyn. *Current Biography 1978*

Florida's favorite centerfold
In October 1979 Burt Reynolds became only the 2nd man to appear on the cover of a famous magazine—but you got me what magazine! Was it. . . ?
1. *Playboy*
2. *Woman's Day*
3. *Cosmopolitan*

In April 1964, Peter Sellers was the 1st man to appear on a *Playboy* cover; Burt Reynolds was 2nd. Reynolds' famous nude centerfold

appeared in *Cosmopolitan* in 1972. *[www.playboy.com] and The Ledger Online (Lakeland) [www.theledger.com]*

🎭 BONUS Burt question

According to Burt Reynolds' personal assistant, Burt lays out $1,500 a week for—you got me! Is it. . . ?
1. Alimony for Loni Anderson
2. Viagra
3. Hairpieces

According to Elaine Blake Hall in 1994, Burt's hairpieces cost $1,500 and he needs a new one every week. *Burt and Me by Elaine Blake Hall*

Black comedy

The 1st African-American actor to get featured billing in a movie was a Key West native whose screen name came from a racehorse on which $30 had been won—but you got me who that was! Was that actor. . . ?
1. Stepin Fetchit
2. Butterfly McQueen
3. Rochester

Born Lincoln Theodore Perry in 1902, Stepin Fetchit's screen roles were studies in the racial stereotypes of the day. *Whatever Became Of. . . ? (8th series)*

The bigger they are

In a 1977 Joan Collins creature feature subtitled "How The Pest Was Won," giant pests menaced a Florida resort and hypnotized the residents—but you got me what kind of pests they were! Were they. . . ?
1. Raccoons
2. Ants
3. Toy poodles

The movie *Empire of the Ants* was based (loosely) on an H. G. Wells story. *Halliwell's Film & Video Guide 1998 and John Stanley's Creature Feature Strikes Again*

All right, Mr. DeMille, I'm ready for my close-up

In 1951 when C. B. DeMille filmed his spectacular *The Greatest Show on Earth* in "Circus City," he hired local Sarasotans as extras—but you

got me how much C. B. paid them! Was it. . . ?
1. **75¢ per hour**
2. **$3.50 per hour**
3. **$5.35 per hour**

75¢. *Quintessential Sarasota by Jeff LaHurd*

Many scenes for the 1941 romantic musical *Moon Over Miami* (WWII pinup Betty Grable and her million-dollar legs go fortune hunting) were shot at a Winter Haven theme park—but you got me which one! Was it. . . ?
1. **Weeki Wachee Springs**
2. **Cypress Gardens**
3. **Marineland**

Cypress Gardens. *Museum of Florida History [www.dos.state.fl.us]*

Stage fright
The monstrous looks of former Tampa resident Rondo Hatton (who suffered from a deforming condition called acromegaly) got him cast as a psycho fiend in a series of monster movies like *House of Horrors* (1946) and *The Spider Woman Strikes Back* (1946). But you got me what role Hatton made famous. Was he. . . ?
1. **The Creeper**
2. **The Man with Two Faces**
3. **It**

Rondo Hatton was The Creeper. *The Weekly Planet May 28–June 6, 1998, and Leonard Maltin's Movie and Video Guide 1993*

This actress, born in 1911 on Central Avenue in Tampa, is best remembered for her role in *Gone with the Wind* when she takes a raincheck as Olivia De Havilland's midwife saying, "I don't know nothin' about birthin' babies." But you got me who she was! Was she. . . ?
1. **Butterfly McQueen**
2. **Vivien Leigh**
3. **Hattie McDaniel**

Thelma "Butterfly" McQueen. *Tampa Tribune 9-25-94 and The Movie Quote Book by Harry Haun*

You Jane

One actress played Jane 6 times to Johnny Weismuller's Tarzan, the last time in 1941, in *Tarzan's Secret Treasure*, which was shot partly in Silver Springs. But you got me who she was! Was she. . . ?
1. O'Sullivan
2. O. Henry
3. O Canada

Maureen O'Sullivan, mother of Mia Farrow, passed away in 1998. Silver Springs is still home to descendants of the monkeys brought there for *Tarzan* episodes. *Museum of Florida History [www.dos.state.fl.us], People 7-6-98, and Some Kind of Paradise by Mark Derr*

Green around the gills

Originally in 3-D, this 1954 monster movie about a Gill Man in the Amazon was filmed partly in Wakulla Springs and Tarpon Springs— but you got me what lagoon that creature supposedly hailed from! Was it. . . ?
1. The Blue Lagoon
2. The Black Lagoon
3. The Black-and-Blue Lagoon

The Creature from the Black Lagoon. Museum of Florida History [www.dos.state.fl.us] and Leonard Maltin's Movie and Video Guide 1993

Jerry Lewis made his directorial debut and starrred in *The Bellboy,* which was set at the same Miami Beach hotel where James Bond found the golden girl Shirley Eaton in *Goldfinger*. But you got me what hotel! Was it. . . ?
1. The Fontainebleau
2. The Eden Roc
3. The Biltmore

A popular Rat Pack playground, today it's the Fontainebleau Hilton. The Fontainebleau was also the setting for the '60s detective series *Surfside Six* and the film *The Bodyguard*. *Hollywood East by Ames Ponti, Rat Pack Confidential by Shawn Levy, and Shot on This Site by William A. Gordon*

🎬 BONUS Fontainebleau/Rat Pack question

On March 26, 1960, the "Frank Sinatra-Timex Show" was taped at the

Fontainebleau for ABC. The special featured the 1st post-Army performance of a legendary singer. But you got me who! Was it. . . ?

1. **Elvis Presley**
2. **Roy Orbison**
3. **Chubby Checker**

For the "Welcome Home, Elvis" special, Elvis sang "Witchcraft" and Sinatra sang "Love Me Tender." *The Billboard Book of Number One Hits by Fred Bronson and Rat Pack Confidential by Shawn Levy*

Beautiful downtown Jacksonville

Jacksonville in the early days was a movie capital to rival Hollywood. Florida's 1st films were 1898 newsreels of U.S. troops bivouacked in Tampa for—you got me what war! Was it. . . ?

1. **The Civil War**
2. **The Spanish-American War**
3. **World War I**

 The Spanish-American War. The newsreels were *U.S. Cavalry Supplies Unloading at Tampa Florida* and *Transport Ships at Port Tampa. Museum of Florida History [www.dos.state.fl.us] and Hollywood East by Ames Ponti*

Chapter 24

It's a Beautiful Day in the Neighborhood— Florida Weather

It's raining, it's pouring

On average, 17 people lose their lives every year in U.S. hurricanes— but you got me how many of those deadly storms the North Atlantic averages every year! Is it. . . ?

1. 1
2. 2–3
3. 6–8

The season runs from June 1 to November 30, and 8 hurricanes are average in the North Atlantic. *St. Petersburg Times 2-25-98*

Lightning strikes more than twice

Annually, the average Florida resident can expect to be within ½ mile of a certain number of lightning bolts that hit the ground—but you got me how many! Is it. . . ?

1. 1–2
2. 5–7
3. 10–15

Ten to fifteen lightning bolts will hit within ½ mile of every Florida resident each year. The state's worst lightning belt extends from Tampa to Orlando, with lightning occurring about two-thirds of summer days. *Florida Weather by Morton D. Winsberg and Knight-Ridder Newspapers 7-9-93*

🏝️ BONUS lightning question

Lightning deaths in Florida hit an all-time one-year high in 1971—but you got me how many poor souls bought the farm! Was it. . . ?

Bathing beauties with a sign illustrating Florida's average daytime temperature, Daytona Beach, 1925

1. 11
2. 19
3. 27

In 1971 lightning killed 19. From 1959–1993, in Florida, 339 people were killed; an average of 10 deaths and 29 injured per year. *Knight-Ridder Newspapers 7-9-93*

'Scuse me while I kiss the sky

From February 9, 1967, to March 17, 1969, St. Petersburg had 768 days in a row of—you got me! Was it. . . ?
1. Days over 90°
2. Rain
3. Sun

The Guinness Book of World Records credits St. Petersburg with 768 consecutive sunny days. In a great 70-year promotion, the *Evening Independent* newspaper in St. Petersburg promised to give away the paper on days when the sun didn't shine. *The Guinness Book of World Records 1998 and St. Petersburg Times 1-12-98*

Your odds of getting hit by a hurricane in Jacksonville in any given year are about 1 in 100, but in Miami and the Keys, they're—you got me! Are they. . . ?
1. Twice that—about 1 in 50
2. About 7 in 100
3. About 14 in 100

Miami and the Keys stand a 14% chance of getting hit with a hurricane in an average year. *Sierra Club Guide to the Natural Areas of Florida by John Perry and Jane Greverus Perry*

How low can you go?

Lower Matecumbe Key has the distinction of recording the lowest one of these in the United States—but you got me what! Is it. . . ?
1. The lowest elevation
2. The lowest per-capita income
3. The lowest barometer reading

The record low barometer reading was 26.35 inches in September 1935. *National Oceanic and Atmospheric Administration 1971*

Those lazy, hazy, crazy days of summer

In July 1984, a dusty haze settled over south Florida—but you got me where that haze blew in from! Was it the. . . ?

1. Sahara Desert
2. Montserrat volcano
3. American Dust Bowl

The dust blew across the ocean from the Sahara. *Florida Weather by Morton D. Winsberg*

Your average hurricane covers an area some 100 miles in diameter. But you got me what the diameter of the average "eye" is! Is it. . . ?

1. 1.5 miles
2. 6 miles
3. 14 miles

Fourteen miles. *National Oceanic and Atmospheric Administration 1971*

BONUS hurricane question

Of the top 5 deadliest hurricanes in the U.S. from 1900 to 1996—you got me how many hit Florida! Was it. . . ?

1. Only 1
2. 3
3. All 5

The 3 were unnamed hurricanes that hit Lake Okeechobee (1,836 dead) in 1928, the Keys in 1919 and again in 1935 (600 and 408 dead, respectively). *Florida Statistical Abstract 1997*

The National Weather Service started doing something to hurricanes in 1953—but you got me what! Was it. . . ?

1. Tracking them
2. Categorizing them as force 1 to force 5
3. Giving them feminine names

In 1953 the NWS adopted the policy to name hurricanes after women. In 1978 eastern north-Pacific storms started getting both men's and women's names; the following year, Atlantic and Gulf of Mexico storms. *U.S. Department of Commerce—NOAA—National Weather Service*

Hey, you, get off my cloud

Every 15 minutes your typical south Florida thunderstorm will produce—you got me how many lightning strikes! Is it. . . ?
1. 10–20
2. 30–40
3. 50–100

**Fifty to one hundred are typical, although 1,000-plus have been
picked up by sensors. (Other numbers exist.)** *Knight-Ridder
Newspapers 7-9-93*

You got me which one is hotter! Is it. . . ?
1. **The sun's surface**
2. **Lightning**
3. **The line for Dumbo at the Magic Kingdom**

**Lightning peaks at about 50,000°, about 4 or 5 times what the sun's
surface is.** *Knight-Ridder Report 7-9-93*

Thanks, but no thanks

Addressing a nationwide gathering of meteorologists at Florida State
in November 1961, Jack Reed of Sandia Laboratory in Albuquerque
discussed a promising way to break up or steer away hurricanes. But
you got me what he suggested! Was it. . . ?
1. **Seeding the clouds to drop their rain out at sea**
2. **Giant turbines to blow them offshore**
3. **Setting off a nuke in the eye**

**He thought that dropping a big nuclear bomb in the eye might do
the trick.** *Tampa Tribune 11-15-61*

You got me what you're afraid of if you suffer from brontophobia! Is
it. . . ?
1. **Tornadoes**
2. **Thunder**
3. **Hurricanes**

**Greek *brontē* means thunder. And should you suffer from brontopho-
bia, the correct saint to invoke is Saint Barbara.** *American Heritage
Dictionary and Encylopedia Britannica*

One of the following statements is true about Hurricanes Quentin, Ulysses,
Xanthus, Yvonne, and Zelda—but you got me which one! Is it. . . ?

1. They were Florida's worst historical storms
2. There were no hurricanes Quentin, Ulysses, Xanthus, Yvonne, and Zelda
3. They are the designated names for the 1st named storms of the 21st century

No such hurricanes. The letters Q, U, X, Y, and Z are not used because there aren't too many names that start with them. *NOAA—National Weather Service*

According to folklore predicting, count the number of times a house cricket chirps in 15 seconds, add 37 to that and you get—you got me! Is it. . . ?
1. How long you'll live
2. The temperature
3. The inches of rain per year

The temperature. *St. Petersburg Times 8-23-81*

Yankeetown, founded in 1905 by the same man who planned Gary, Indiana, holds the nation's record for—you got me! Is it. . . ?
1. Highest temperature
2. Lowest elevation below sea level
3. Rainfall

Yankeetown got a record rainfall of 38.7 inches in 24 hours in 1950. By contrast, the Keys only average 40 inches in a year. *Florida Handbook 1997–1998*

What happened was just this: the wind began to switch
Florida tornadoes occur most commonly in the spring and summer, and about—you got me what time of day! Is it. . . ?
1. Around dawn
2. In the afternoon and early evening
3. In the dead of night

Afternoons and early evenings are most common. However, the twisters that ripped through the Orlando area in February 1998 came around midnight and were the deadliest tornadoes in Florida since the National Weather Service began keeping records. *Tampa Tribune 2-24-98 and St. Petersburg Times 2-25-98*

Come for the beaches, stay for the tobogganing
The biggest ones in Florida happened on the same date, February 13th, in the years 1899 and 1958—but you got me what! Were they. . . ?
1. Snowfalls
2. Hurricanes
3. Bank robberies

Snowfalls. *Florida Handbook 1997–1998*

A bolt from the blue
In Florida more people get struck by lightning while—you got me! Is it. . . ?
1. On or in the water
2. In open fields or playgrounds
3. Under trees

Twenty-eight percent of lightning deaths and injuries happen in open fields or playgrounds; 26% in or on the water; 10% under trees. *Florida Weather by Morton D. Winsberg*

Sweatin' with the oldies
June 29, 1931, saw the all-time record high temperature in the state—but you got me what it was! Was it. . . ?
1. 104°
2. 109°
3. 113°

The record high set at Monticello is 109°. The record low was -2° at Tallahassee in 1899. *Florida Handbook 1997–1998*

Since 1900 Florida averages about 1 major hurricane every 4 years. But since the year 1966 there have only been—you got me! Is it. . . ?
1. 3
2. 6
3. 9

Eloise in 1975, Elena in 1985, and Andrew in 1992. *Florida Handbook 1997–1998*

In August 1992 the costliest storm in history, Hurricane Andrew, caused losses estimated at—you got me! Was it. . . ?

1. $27 million
2. $2.7 billion
3. $27 billion

 $27 billion in losses; 44 people lost their lives. *Florida Handbook 1997–1998*

Chapter 25

It's Not the Heat, It's the Stupidity—Florida Odds and Ends

20/20 vision

On April 4, 1991, ABC's *20/20* magazine show aired footage of something being done to a 16-year old Florida girl named Gina—but you got me what! Was she shown being. . . ?
1. Exorcised
2. Crowned Miss Teen USA
3. Married to serial killer Ted Bundy

Two Roman Catholic priests performed the rite of exorcism on the girl. *Facts on File 4-11-91*

One Hillsborough County town was named for and settled by followers of an English art critic and philosopher, whom they used to contact by using a Ouija board. But you got me what town! Is it. . . ?
1. Ruskin
2. Thoreau
3. Glen Ellyn

Ruskin was founded by John Ruskin–follower Dr. George Miller, who tried to build a town around a college with a Christian–Socialist bent. *Tampa Tribune 7-10-85*

On a roll

On 5th Street in Lake Wales, there's a strange place where you can stop your car at the bottom of hill, stick it in neutral, let the brake off and—voila!—your car will appear to defy gravity and roll backward UP the hill! But you got me what that place is called! Is it. . . ?

1. Monback Hill
2. Sasparilla Hilla
3. Spook Hill

Spook Hill. It's an optical illusion, of course, but legends persist involving old Indian ghosts and pirate spirits. *St. Petersburg Times 8-8-75*

In the middle of busy Canova Drive in New Smyrna Beach, there's the grave of 16-year-old Charles Dummett, who was the victim of a hunting accident in 1860. His father was a Hall-of-Famer—but you got me which hall of fame! Was it. . . ?
1. The Citrus Hall of Fame
2. The Baseball Hall of Fame
3. The Ripley's Believe It or Not Hall of Fame

Douglas Dummett, Charles's father, grafted sweet orange buds onto wild orange trees, establishing the prized Indian River oranges. He's credited with being the "Father of the Indian River Citrus Industry" in the Citrus Hall of Fame. *Tampa Tribune 4-25-71 and Some Kind of Paradise by Mark Derr*

Where the sun don't shine
In 1890 a group of followers of Dr. Cyrus Reed Teed established a "New Jerusalem" in Estero to practice the religion of Koreshan Universology. In addition to believing that the Earth was a hollow sphere and we all lived on its inner, concave surface, the Koreshans believed that the sun was—you got me! Was the sun. . . ?
1. Heaven
2. Bright on one side, dark on the other
3. Headed toward us like an asteroid

Koreshans believed the sun had a dark side. The last of the Koreshans, Miss Hedwig Michel, died at 90 in the restored village called Koreshan Unity in Estero in 1982. *Tampa Tribune 8-16-82*

Yo quiero Art Bell
The small town of Bardin reportedly has its own "Bigfoot" wandering around in the woods. The hairy creature is called—you got me! Is he called. . . ?

1. Sugar
2. Booger
3. Meshuge

The Bardin Booger is said to be 6 to 8 feet tall, with footprints 14 to 18 inches long, and a real stinker. The town of Ochopee, east of Naples, is home to another hairy swamp thing known as the skunk ape. *Backroads of Florida by Ann Ruff, St. Petersburg Times 9-18-98, and Real Florida by Jeff Klinkenberg*

Disappearing act
According to Lloyds of London, of the 70 merchant ships that vanished during the decade from 1961 to 1971, the number of those lost in the mysterious Bermuda Triangle was—you got me! Was it. . . ?
1. Only 1
2. 9
3. All but 3

Nine went missing in the Triangle. In March 1866 the Swedish ship *Lotta,* bound out of Göteborg for Havana, became the 1st ship to vanish. The disappearance of 5 Navy torpedo bombers on a training flight from the Naval Air Station at Fort Lauderdale on December 5, 1945, remains one of the most baffling mysteries of the Triangle. *This Baffling World by John Godwin; Florida's Past, Vol. 2 by Gene M. Burnett; St. Petersburg Times 11-13-77; and The People's Almanac by David Wallenchinsky and Irving Wallace*

George Colby got directions from Seneca and followed them to the central Florida woods, where he founded of the town of Cassadaga— but you got me who or what Seneca was! Was Seneca. . . ?
1. A famed New York astrologer
2. One of Colby's "split" personalities
3. An Indian spirit guide

Seneca, an Indian spirit, came to Colby during a séance and described the promised land to him. Cassadaga is still known as a spiritualist center of mediums and readers. *St. Petersburg Times 10-25-81*

Not with the June Taylor Dancers
The "Great One" Jackie Gleason, who relocated his CBS Saturday night variety show to Miami Beach and lived in Lauderhill, died on June 24, 1987, and was buried at St. Mary's Cemetery in Miami. But

you got me what phrase associated with Gleason is on his tombstone! Is it. . . ?

1. "And away we go"
2. "To the moon, Alice"
3. "How sweet it is"

 "And away we go." It was Orson Welles who pinned "the Great One" on Gleason. *[www.findagrave.com] and [www.bibliomag.com]*

And for those of you who can't get enough . . .

For Further Reading
(selected by the Reference Department of the State Library of Florida)

Apalachee: The Land Between the Rivers by John H. Hann (University Press of Florida, 1988)

Archaeology of Precolumbian Florida by Jerald T. Milanich (University Press of Florida, 1994)

Florida: A Short History by Michael V. Gannon (University Press of Florida, 1993)

Florida Cowman: A History of Florida Cattle Raising by Joe A. Akerman (Jimbob Printing, 1989)

Florida's Past: People and Events that Shaped the State, Volumes 1, 2, and 3 by Gene M. Burnett (Pineapple Press, 1988)

History of Florida by Charlton W. Tebeau (University of Miami Press, 1981)

History of the Second Seminole War, 1835–1842 by John K. Mahon (University Press of Florida, 1991, ©1967)

Indian Mounds of the Atlantic Coast: A Guide to Sites from Maine to Florida by Jerry N. McDonald and Susan L. Woodward (out of print)

Yesterday's Florida by Nixon Smiley (out of print)

A Selection of the Author's Favorite Florida Books:

Boone's Florida Historical Markers and Sites by Floyd E. Boone (Rainbow Books, 1987)

Cry of the Panther by James P. McMullen (Pineapple Press, 1996)

Dreamers, Schemers and Scalwags, The Florida Chronicles, Vol. 1 by Stuart B. McIver (Pineapple Press, 1994)

The Everglades: River of Grass by Marjory Stoneman Douglas (Pineapple Press, 1997)

The Florida Handbook 1997–1998 by Allen Morris and Joan Perry Morris (Peninsular Books, 1997)

Florida Ramble by Alex Shoumatoff (out of print)

Miami 1909: with excerpts from Fannie Clemons' diary by Thelma Peters (out of print)

Murder in the Tropics, The Florida Chronicles, Vol. 2 by Stuart B. McIver (Pineapple Press, 1995)

Some Kind of Paradise: A Chronicle of Man and the Land in Florida by Mark Derr (University Press of Florida, 1998)

Up for Grabs: A Trip Through Time and Space in the Sunshine State by John Rothchild (out of print)

The WPA Guide to Florida: The Federal Writer's Project Guide to 1930's Florida (out of print)

Index

Here are some other books from Pineapple Press on related topics. For a complete catalog, write to Pineapple Press, P.O. Box 3899, Sarasota, Florida 34230-3899, or call (800) 746-3275. Or visit our Web site at www.pineapplepress.com.

Cry of the Panther by James McMullen. ISBN 1-56164-118-9 (PB)

Dreamers, Schemers and Scalawags, The Florida Chronicles, Volume 1 by Stuart B. McIver. ISBN 1-56164-155-3 (PB)

The Everglades: River of Grass by Marjory Stoneman Douglas. ISBN 1-56164-135-9 (HB)

Florida Fun Facts by Eliot Kleinberg. ISBN 1-56164-068-9 (PB)

Florida Place Names: Alachua to Zolfo Springs by Allen Morris; Joan Perry Morris, photo editor. ISBN 1-56164-084-0 (HB)

Florida Puzzle Book by Donna Lugg Pape, Virginia Mueller, and Carol Karle. ISBN 1-56164-107-3 (PB)

Florida's Editorial Cartoonists by S. L. Harrison. ISBN 1-56164-108-1 (PB)

Florida's Past: People and Events that Shaped the State, Volumes 1, 2, and 3 by Gene M. Burnett. ISBN 1-56164-115-4 (Volume 1; PB); 1-56164-139-1 (Volume 2; PB); 1-56164-117-0 (Volume 3; PB)

Murder in the Tropics, The Florida Chronicles, Volume 2 by Stuart B. McIver. ISBN 1-56164-079-4 (PB)

The Sunshine State Almanac and Book of Florida-Related Stuff by Phil Philcox and Beverly Boe. ISBN 1-56164-178-2 (PB)